Sleep Paralysis:

A Guide to Hypnagogic Visions & Visitors of the Night

By Ryan Hurd

Hyena Press
Los Altos, CA
www.HyenaPress.com

This book is published by Hyena Press.
2310 Homestead Rd, C1 #125
Los Altos, CA
www.HyenaPress.com

Printed and bound in the United States of America.

Although the author and publisher have made every effort to
ensure the accuracy and completeness of information contained
in this book, we assume no responsibility for errors, inaccuracies,
omissions, or any inconsistency herein. Any slights on people,
places, or organizations are unintentional.

First Paperback Edition
ISBN 978-0-9842239-1-6

Book Design: Justin Oefelein
Editing: Liza Joseph

Illustrations:
Part I - Original illustration for Jonathan Swift's *Gulliver's
Travels* by E. C. Broch, 1894.
Part II - "One summer's evening they went with Bianca
Maria deep into the forest" by John Baeur, 1913.
Illustration for *The Changeling* by Helena Nyblom in the
anthology *Among pixies and trolls*.
Part III - "Queen Katherine's Dream" by William Blake, 1925.

ATTENTION CORPORATIONS, UNIVERSITIES,
COLLEGES, PROFESSIONAL, ORGANIZATIONS—
DISCOUNT ON BULK PURCHASES AVAILABLE.

For information, please contact the publisher:
www.HyenaPress.com, info@hyenapress.com, (408) 329-4597

Acknowledgements

This book is the fruit of my personal struggles with the creatures of sleep paralysis, so first and foremost I want to thank them and my dream allies for blessing me with this ancient and powerful way of knowing.

Back on Middle Earth, I want to thank Scott Sparrow, Robert Waggoner, and especially my wife Wendy for editing and proofreading. I benefited mightily from the wisdom and encouragement of my colleague Jorge Conesa Sevilla. My readers of dreamstudies.org also deserve attention for their brave acts of sharing. This small book also rests upon the lifetime work of David Hufford, who is the first modern researcher to respect the tales of sleep paralysis visions and the people who are courageous enough to tell them.

And a special thank you to the Bishop Pine guardians of Inverness, California, whose forested trails I paced while drafting this project in the winter of 2009.

Dedication

I dedicate this book to my aunt Rachael Jean Walter, who taught me to laugh at myself and gain strength from facing my fears.

Table of Contents

Foreword

Over the course of almost 40 years of involvement in dream research and education, I have lectured to hundreds of audiences on various dream-related subjects. No matter where I go, I hear the same questions over and over again. Some of the questions are easily answered, but some have thus far remained beyond the scope of my ability to provide a succinct and useful answer.

Until meeting Ryan Hurd and learning about his research on sleep paralysis, I would cringe inwardly every time I was asked, "What does it mean when I wake up and can't move? And who is that scary person who appears beside my bed?" I had some ideas, but my answer always ended with, "We really don't understand this phenomenon very well." But now, I have an answer. After reading this book, I can finally say that someone has finally lifted the veil on this strange and often disturbing experience.

The problem with such a complex experience, as Ryan so eloquently points out, is that it partakes of several influences at the same time. Instead of reducing SP and its attendant nightmare phenomena to a single source, he lays out a multi-dimensional approach. The reader comes to understand that several forces converge simultaneously to create a "dream" that is apparently superimposed on one's physical surroundings. As such, the reader learns about several "feeds" that contribute to the final experience, including the particular physiological condition of the body at the time, as well as the dreamer's own beliefs and fears. By focusing on the importance of modifying the physiological state of the body through dietary and behavioral changes, Ryan establishes that the dreamer can take proactive measures to minimize the frequency or severity of SP symptoms. Further, by emphasizing the influence of the dreamer's emotional state, Ryan establishes that the dreamer can alter the outcome considerably by working on belief, attitude, and expectation.

This approach reflects a cutting-edge orientation to dreams and other visionary experiences, in which the witness's beliefs, attitudes, and responses to the dream effectively co-create the outcome. In the spirit of this "constructivist" perspective, Ryan makes a compelling case that the SP experience is neither good nor bad, but becomes pleasant or unpleasant largely on the basis of what the dreamer brings to it. If we bring fear to it, then it will predictably turn into our worst nightmare. But if we can enter the experience with a calm and courageous heart, then the experience can usher us into lucid dreaming and, potentially, into unimagined states of bliss.

While this book lays out a thorough theoretical approach to the SP phenomenon, it also presents an array of well-researched strategies for modifying the dreamer's physiological and psychological state so that he or she can actually benefit from and take advantage of the SP experience. As such, Ryan's approach represents an altogether practical and refreshing alternative to the uninformed belief that SP indicates an objective threat or psychological dysfunction.

Most importantly, this book is the product of Ryan's own struggle to understand and benefit from his SP experiences. Through his own extensive experience with sleep paralysis, Ryan Hurd has turned lead into gold, and now, he has gold to share.

-**Gregory Scott Sparrow**, *Ed.D, LPC*
Author of *Lucid Dreaming: Dawning of the Clear Light*
January 7, 2010

Introduction

The American Psychological Association defines sleep paralysis as the "brief inability to move or speak just before falling asleep or on awakening... accompanied by hallucinations."[1] This harmless period of immobility, derived from muscle paralysis or *atonia*, happens every night as a natural side effect of dreaming sleep. But, when we become self-aware of this process, the trouble begins. Be it by accident or design, these brief episodes can come with powerful dream-like hallucinations that are projected, like a 3D movie, into the space of our sleeping quarters. Together, this paralysis and its associated visions are a misunderstood aspect of the human visionary capability that cause many people undue stress and shame.

Sleep paralysis nightmares are still a mystery to medical science, even though 40% of the world's population reports having these experiences at least once in their lives.[2] Among college students, three out of four have experienced sleep paralysis with hallucinations.[3] Despite this widespread occurrence, people typically react to this naturally occurring vision state with terror, confusion, and, too often, silence.

Let me say it plainly. If you have had Sleep Paralysis (SP) and, upon awakening, see people who aren't really there, trust that you are not suffering a psychotic breakdown. Nor are you necessarily haunted by ghosts or malevolent entities, which is the historical and folk explanation for this phenomenon. The visions that accompany SP feel as real as waking life because they are actually occurring in a state of mind that is part dream-vision and part physical reality. This guide not only explains the current theories about the origins of these visions, but also gives practical tactics for preventing them from happening again. And finally, this guide provides a roadmap that will assist you in transforming these unwanted nightmares into extraordinary dreams, as sleep paralysis can become a gift for dreamers who are open to the mysteries of the mind.

A quick note about ghosts, goblins, and demons: those who are open to their SP experiences sometimes come into contact with "archetypal" entities with their own agendas that appear to be associated with the local landscape, as well as certain homes and historical locations. It is as if these encounters hold memories for the location by playing out myths that can be traumatic or ecstatic for the SP visionary. These experiences can also bring up information that dreamers confirm later from other sources, such as historical documents or testimonials from long-term residents. At the very least, this uncanny side of SP visions is a shocking reminder of the value of non-rational realms and our incomplete scientific paradigm of the natural world. But while the context of many terrifying SP hallucinations have a "paranormal" air to them, it is not the aim of this book to pass judgment on the reality of spirits. To explore SP and its visions, we need open hearts and minds, and this factor is often missing in the paranormal explanations of SP encounters.

Rather, I start by addressing the *psychological* reality of spirits: these visions feel real, they are not a dream in the usual sense of the word, and they can instigate real life changes that linger far beyond the terror of that night. The primary focus of this book is on how to prepare the dreamer/visionary to successfully navigate this bizarre realm without fear. This book is a training manual, not a manifesto.

My Story

I have personally struggled with isolated sleep paralysis. I experienced my first encounter twenty years ago, when I was 14 years old. Here's what I wrote (verbatim) in my journal at the time:

> *"I'm standing around and the phone rings. I went to pick it up and heard this voice—a voice I never want to hear again. It said, "Darkness rules!" Then, there was a smell --no an atmosphere-- of evil and I felt I was being dragged down into something. It was like being pushed. I forced myself to wake up. I was sweating like a hog. I looked around my room and thought it was over. Suddenly, that pushing sensation started again while I was WIDE AWAKE! Whatever the hell it was (probably was hell), it was pushing me back down to sleep. I don't mean that I felt a bit tired and closed my eyes ---it was literally shoving me asleep...."*

I didn't find out for several years that this was a textbook example of a SP nightmare. I thought I was haunted by demons, but I was too embarrassed to tell anyone because it sounded crazy. But I knew what I experienced felt *real* because I was awake when it happened.

Even long after I discovered the name of this condition, I was still disturbed by occasional bouts of sleep paralysis. My nightmares kept me up at night, and this affected my daily life. I walked around with a haunted look. Eventually, I decided I had to find a way to deal with my nightmares. So I studied dream science and learned everything I could about "conscious dreams" and nightmares.

Over time, I learned not only how to reduce my SP nightmares, but also how to swallow my fear and regain self-control in the nightmare itself. And thanks to a few wise teachers in my life, I came to see how these visions are a gateway to powerful and exhilarating dreams that renewed my optimism and hope for the future.

My hope is that readers will learn quickly how to dance in this strange and mystical world without worry and learn in measured stages what I learned haltingly through trial and error.

Roadmap

This book is divided into three parts: *Coping with Sleep Paralysis*, *Confronting Apparitions*, and *Thriving with Sleep Paralysis*.

Part I is a practical guide for those who wish to stop having SP and take control when it does happen. It contains tips that will help you break SP that very night. These are tactics to employ while you are in paralysis so you can wake up immediately. Next, we'll turn to lifestyle changes that can lessen susceptibility to SP. These tactics are mostly about changing certain habits, which takes most people about two weeks to cement into practice. Finally, Part I addresses the psychological aspects of SP, including how to get grounded and let go of fear.

Part II is focused on the apparitions that occur in one out of five SP experiences. First, we will review current theories about how apparitions form and what they have to say. These terrifying visions are the most misunderstood aspect of SP. Next, we will review the forms the apparitions may take and provide some concrete strategies for preventing them from escalating into nightmares. Sometimes, the SP apparition or "Stranger" can lead you on a journey to self-discovery. In fact, this Stranger is also connected to a long history of helpful figures, such as spirit guides, angels, and ancestors. This section gives practical advice about exploring these intriguing possibilities.

Part III is a guide to thriving with SP. This section includes advanced dreaming techniques that are possible once you have mastered the lessons in Part I and II. Effective tactics are covered for inducing out-of-body experiences, lucid dreams, and hypnagogic reverie, all of which can be accessed from SP. The last chapter in Part III teaches how courageous dreamers can increase the odds of SP in order to access extraordinary dreams and visions on purpose.

Medical Disclaimer

I am not a medical doctor, and this book is only for educational purposes. Also, the tactics included here should not be considered a substitution for medical or psychological treatment. Normally, isolated sleep paralysis is not considered harmful, unless exhibited symptoms include sleep apnea, narcolepsy, or other related parasomas.[4] Some of these other symptoms include excessive sleepiness, severe insomnia, the inability to sleep because of breathing difficulties, and cataplexy (paralysis in the daytime triggered by sudden emotion). If you are unsure—even a little unsure—that you experience some of these symptoms, I encourage you to make an appointment with a sleep specialist.

Also, consider taking a free anonymous sleep disorder test on the Internet. I recommend the University of Maryland's sleep disorder test online.

Repetitive isolated sleep paralysis (RISP) is also correlated with panic disorder and Post-Traumatic Stress Disorder.[5] If high levels of anxiety and/or disturbing flashbacks are occurring in waking life, as well as in your sleep paralysis hallucinations, I recommend seeing a mental health care provider in your area. Many cities provide free access to evaluations, and other counselors provide their services on a sliding-scale.

A Note about Terminology

I often use *Sleep Paralysis* (SP) and *Isolated Sleep Paralysis* (iSP) interchangeably in this book. In both cases, I am referring to isolated sleep paralysis.

Also, I use the term *hypnagogic hallucinations* (HH) to include both hypnagogic ("upon going to sleep") as well as hypnopompic ("upon waking up") imagery.

Part I:
Beating Sleep Paralysis

CHAPTER ONE
Tactics For Breaking The Paralysis

If you are suffering, read this chapter first because it will make a difference tonight. The most important thing to know upfront is that isolated sleep paralysis (ISP) is a natural part of sleep, even though it feels alarming. This chapter reviews the symptoms of SP and then goes over the most effective methods to wake up immediately and gain self-control.

Symptoms of Isolated Sleep Paralysis

The symptoms of SP are nearly universal and have been noted throughout history and across cultures. However, not everyone has *all* the sensations below.

- *Being unable to move*
- *Feeling like being held down or experiencing a great weight pushing down on your chest, abdomen, or throat*
- *Hearing strange sounds like buzzing or a crackling paper bag*
- *Hearing voices, such as your own name being called*
- *Feeling like gravity is shifting around or that you are floating or sinking*
- *Experiencing difficulty in breathing*
- *Pounding heart*
- *Experiencing extreme fear and terror, followed by strong emotions after it's over*

- *Having an out-of-body experience*
- *Feeling slight electrical currents all over the body, especially in the head*
- *Experiencing powerful "boom"-like electrical shocks*
- *Seeing spiders, insects, or other creepy-crawlies all over the room*
- *Feeling a "presence" in the room, like someone is watching you*
- *Seeing an apparition in the room, often a nightmarish or mythological figure*
- *Being touched by the apparition during SP*
- *Feeling all of the above as "more real than real," accompanied by full awareness*

The "attack" usually lasts a minute or two, but some people have reported attacks lasting over an hour.[6] Afterwards, many people are exhausted, covered in sweat and afraid to go back to sleep. Some have palpitations and may tremble and shake from the fear. Multiple attacks during the same night are commonplace, causing the sufferer to lose an entire night of sleep, as well as causing extreme emotional fatigue. This is often diagnosed as Repetitive Isolated Sleep Paralysis (RISP) and can be treated with prescription medications. Examples really bring the range of SP into focus. Here are some SP attacks anonymously recorded at DreamStudies.org.

> *I woke and couldn't move. I could feel/see someone was in the room: terrible!*

> *I felt terrified, and there was pressure on me – I couldn't move – I felt I was awake.*

> *There was some type of force holding me back – I couldn't really move and could not breath. I saw myself trying to scream and reach out for help but couldn't. I woke up gasping for air.*

> *I couldn't move. I had this sharp loud radio static in my right ear.*

Awake, I was held at knife-point while he attacked me. I fought while he tried to rape me.

I felt like I was being crushed.

Trapped inside of myself, trying to cry out, trying to get more air. It's always frightening, and usually, I feel a sense of evil with me.

One time, I thought the Devil was standing over my bed, trying to get me... I was paralyzed.

Causes of Isolated Sleep Paralysis

In general, iSP is caused by a disrupted sleep schedule, social stress, and life anxiety, as well as lifestyle choices that can aggravate stress and insomnia.

Here's a more in-depth list of the contributing causes of iSP:

- Insomnia and sleep deprivation
- An erratic sleep schedule
- Jet lag
- Sleeping on your back
- Stress, such as work-related social anxiety or financial anxiety
- Major life changes, such as loss, a relationship breakup, or relocation
- Overuse of stimulants, such as coffee, soda, and black tea
- Physical fatigue
- Having a diagnosed panic disorder
- Certain medications, such as for ADHD
- A history of childhood sexual abuse
- A crisis of faith or search for meaning (Also known as "spiritual emergency")

Tactics to Break Sleep Paralysis Tonight

Below are the best tactics to break SP tonight. Because this is such a personal thing, some of these will work for you, and others won't. Choose the ones that make the most sense to you intuitively. At the end of the book, you can fill out the *Sleep Paralysis Worksheet* to reinforce what you've learned and design your own SP management plan.

Don't Fight

If you feel like you are being held down and you can't move, do not fight back. This actually will intensify the experience. Not only is fighting back likely to increase the feeling of being held down (so much that it may seem like you are being crushed), but fighting back will also increase fear, thus triggering the emotional centers of the brain and strengthening the nightmare.[7] Controlling fear is the most important skill to develop for handling these moments.

Surrender and Go with the Flow

Instead of resisting, try to relax when you notice SP starting to happen. Prepare an affirmation like "This is SP and I am okay." If you feel pressure on your chest, see if you can go with the pressure rather than against it. It's like winning a fight by having no resistance. For example, I often feel like I'm being pushed into the mattress when I have SP. I let myself go and mentally pull in the direction I am being pushed. What happens is I then pop into a full-on dream, or I can wake up directly.

Wiggle Your Toe

Another effective tactic that works for many people is to try to move an extremity, such as a finger or a toe. Most feelings of paralysis are in the belly, chest, and throat. So focus all your attention on the toe and try to move it back and forth. In many cases, this will break the paralysis.

Clench Your Fist

This is a variation of the toe wiggle method. Clench and unclench your fist. Also, I have had success with Jeremy Taylor's method of scrunching up the face muscles, like making a face after smelling something unpleasant.

Focus on Your Breath

An easy way to stop these nightmares is to do some controlled breathing. Controlled breathing does several things at once. For starters, it lessens the feelings of chest pain that sometimes accompany SP. Breathing is autonomic like the heart's beating or digestion, so it's not paralyzed like the big muscles in our arms, chest, and legs. But breath can be controlled with attention or be affected by severe fear, which may be why SP sufferers "forget" to breathe when under attack. *If you can control your breath, you can control your fear.* Simply draw your breath in at a normal rate and exhale fully, using all of your lung capacity. Notice that you can breathe fully without obstruction. This technique will keep you calm as the SP runs its course, and then, you will wake up without any trouble. A few moments of focused breathing with a strong intention to wake up is effective. I discuss the role of breath in greater depth in Chapter 7.

Lean into Love to Find Courage

Now is also the time to lean into unconditional love. For many, the surest path is in religious or spiritual beliefs. Focus on a figure whom you admire and love. Think of someone who calms you down—someone who you associate with peace, love, and safety. This could be Jesus, the Dali Lama, or someone you know personally. In my first SP nightmare when I was fourteen years old, I thought about the love and respect I had for a girl in my class. Embarrassing to admit, yes. But the feelings of oppression and evil dissipated immediately. In this case, true love really does conquer all.

Getting Help from Your Sleep Partner

If someone shares your bed, you can tell them about your SP attacks and what to look for when you are having a nightmare. For example, my wife used to shake me awake whenever I began to breath heavily and irregularly in my sleep. As it turned out, she was waking me up each and every time from an intense SP nightmare. Now, when this happens, I tell her not to wake me up because I actually use SP to go into a lucid dream (as I discuss in Chapter 6).

You could also have your partner respond to a verbal request. This only works some of the time because some people cannot speak in paralysis. But some can. Choose a short word that is easy to say. "Help" is a good choice. When you're in paralysis, focus your attention on your throat and say "Help." Don't try to say it as loud as you can; what may happen is that your imagination will take over and you will only say the word in your dream. Instead, say it forcefully, without screaming.

Coughing for Help

A variation of using your voice is to try to cough into wakefulness. Like breathing, coughing can be autonomic or consciously regulated. By coughing on purpose, you can jar yourself awake or attract the attention of someone nearby. Keep in mind that this method may result in false awakening, which I'll describe below.

Beware of False Awakenings

False awakenings are dreams that seem like waking life, and they are common with SP. They are alarming because we think we are awake, but then suddenly, a new nightmare occurs. Some people have five to ten false awakenings in a row, and when they finally wake up for real, they are harried and may even doubt their sanity. Not only do we feel awake during the experience, but the dream is modeled to look just like our actual sleeping space. Only after awakening "again" do we realize that we were still dreaming.

My rule of thumb is that if I am questioning whether or not

I am dreaming or awake, chances are I'm dreaming. Pinching yourself is not effective because you can feel pain in a dream. The best thing to do is to walk into another room. Going through a threshold like this often shows the dream for what it is, as the next room won't be your hallway but some other bizarre scene. If this is the case—congratulations, you are lucid dreaming and you can safely explore!

Also, testing your memory can determine if you are dreaming or not. Dreams in REM sleep make it difficult to access some kinds of memories. Try to remember your name, your current address. and what you had for dinner last night. If you cannot remember, you are probably dreaming.

When you are sure you're dreaming and do not want to explore the dream, try closing your eyes and doing some deep breathing, and then, open your eyes as hard as you can.

Breaking Repetitive SP

Paralysis nightmares are notorious for recurring several times in a night. Even if you wake up all the way and get out of bed, sometimes they come back as you settle back down to sleep. A warning: some of these methods will make it difficult for you to go back to sleep, but at least you'll be emotionally centered and not scared to go back to bed. Do the exercises below, and then, use your normal relaxation techniques for going to bed, such as reading or listening to music (see Chapter 2 for more techniques).

Bright Light
When you wake up, turn on the light and look at it for at least a minute. This will reset the body's natural clock (the circadian rhythm) and lessen the chance of a repeat later in the night.

Do 10 minutes of Exercise
The absolute best thing to do immediately after a paralysis nightmare is to get out of bed and do some exercise that raises your

heart rate for five to ten minutes. Do some yoga, use the treadmill, climb your stairs, whatever works. This method also helps with refreshing your emotional balance after a scary dream.

Journal the Encounter

Writing down what happened can give the encounter some perspective and distance. Pay attention to your emotions, your responses while in SP, and any hallucinations you remember. Keeping a journal can also help you notice patterns over time, such as when SP occurs and how your reaction changes as you gain familiarity with the state.

Summary of Chapter One: A 5-Step Method

Too many tactics can be overwhelming, so here is a five-step method that has proven effective for hundreds of sufferers of iSP. This method was developed by Fariba Bogzaran,[8] a somatic psychologist and dream researcher.

1. Identify that you are in SP. Tell yourself, "I realize I am in SP."
2. Do not struggle. Instead, relax and let go of negative thoughts.
3. Focus on your breath while you relax.
4. Wait patiently and keep your awareness.
5. Observe if a new dream comes which you can follow or wake yourself up from.

Make a Plan

Again, not every tactic will work with you. It is important to design a strategy, almost like the fire escape plan you may have for evacuating your family home in case of emergency.

Fill out *Sleep Paralysis Worksheet* now to design your plan. Writing it down will reinforce the most important aspects of taking control of SP so that you can get some quality sleep and move beyond the fearful aspects of the encounter.

CHAPTER TWO
Getting Better Sleep

This chapter includes tactics and advice for reducing insomnia, which may be the single greatest cause of isolated SP. Some of these tactics will be helpful tonight, while others may take some time to implement.

Having fears about going back to sleep is a common symptom of repetitive SP. It's a vicious circle because one of the leading causes of SP is not having enough sleep in the first place. Taking a good, hard look at your sleep life, or *sleep hygiene*, is crucial to ridding yourself of these terrifying episodes in the middle of the night.

The problem is really threefold:
1) not getting enough sleep in general
2) not getting enough quality sleep, and
3) having erratic sleep patterns.

If you can improve your sleep hygiene by getting more and better rest and observing a bedtime schedule, you may be able to kick SP within a couple weeks.

Before moving on to some easy ways to improve your sleep life, let's take a quick look at some recent findings about the science of sleep, especially as it concerns SP and insomnia.

The Science of Sleep Paralysis

Sleep paralysis was not understood by the medical establishment until recently. The experiences of thousands of sufferers were thought to be folklore and were lumped together with other kinds of nightmares. Finally, in the 1970s, several sleep laboratories studied patients who suffered nightly from SP. Since then, we have learned a lot about the biology of isolated sleep paralysis and its effect on the mind and body.

Understanding the Physical Mechanisms Behind SP

- SP occurs during an intrusion of rapid-eye movement (REM) sleep into sleep-onset and light sleep (stage 1 and stage 2 sleep).[9] REM is the stage of sleep when dreaming normally occurs.
- The paralysis is physically real due to the weakening of muscle tone in voluntary muscle groups (the somatic nervous system). Normally, this prevents us from acting out the behaviors that we envision during dreaming sleep. In the case of SP, the dreamer has paralysis during sleep onset and sometimes when waking up out of dreaming sleep and becomes conscious of the muscle atonia. This is the physical cause of the feelings of oppression, weight, and the inability to move.
- SP sufferers sometimes open their eyes during these sensations, taking in real information about where they are sleeping. However, most of the time, the eyes are closed despite the seeming "reality" of seeing and hearing the outside environment. The boundary is unclear.
- REM imagery (dream-like imagery and sounds) can simultaneously merge with this real-time sensing, creating terrifying combinations of the dream world and the waking world. These visions are called *hypnagogic hallucinations*. Hypnagogia is a term that simply means "leading into sleep."

Sleep Paralysis and Insomnia

Even though SP happens to most people only once or twice in their lives, the chances of experiencing it drastically increase if you don't get enough sleep or if your sleep patterns are erratic. That's precisely why there is a higher-than-average population of SP sufferers in occupations and lifestyles, such as:

- Truck and taxi drivers
- Doctors, nurses, and other medical personnel
- College students
- Factory workers on the graveyard shift
- Any job that requires sleep habits to be changed often (flexible shifts)
- Parenting a newborn baby

Why is insomnia linked with SP? Sleep scientists suggest that the root cause may be REM-sleep deprivation.[10] When we don't get enough REM sleep, a rebound effect occurs, and the next time we lie down, we will spend more time in REM than usual. REM (and the dreams that come with it) can also appear at strange times, such as during quick naps and right after going to bed at night.

Some people can work long, erratic hours without any harm. But not all of us can. If you just switched jobs and started encountering SP, you may find the symptoms decrease as your body adjusts to your new lifestyle.

While it may not be feasible to get seven or eight hours of unbroken sleep, there are still ways to get the most out of your sleep life. The rest of this chapter is dedicated to ways of improving your sleep hygiene as a way to repel SP and other kinds of nightmares.

Taking Control of your Sleep Hygiene

Schedule Your Sleep Life
An erratic sleep schedule multiplies the likelihood of

experiencing iSP. Even if you work the graveyard shift, you can beat SP by sticking to a regular bedtime and wake-up call. Shift workers and nursing moms will have the hardest time with this, but the other tips in this chapter can help make up the difference.

We are habitual creatures, and our sleep life is ruled by a mechanism known as the circadian rhythm or the *diurnal clock*. The average human has a diurnal clock that resets every 25 hours or so, slightly longer than the solar day. This "clock" is really a schedule of various brain chemicals that determine when we are most alert and when we should sleep. The clock is used to a little give-and-take, but when we do not go to bed at a usual time for an extended period, our energy levels can be seriously compromised, bringing on a range of problems, including immune system depletion, memory problems, and sleep disorders, such as SP.

To alleviate the cause of diurnal clock malfunctions, go to bed around the same time each night, and wake up around the same time each morning. This takes a little discipline at first, but observing a regular sleep schedule is the quickest way to cure SP and nightmares.

If you want to catch up on sleep on the weekends, it's better for your circadian rhythms to go to bed a little earlier and wake up at the usual time. Of course, weekends are great for late night socializing. My advice: Let yourself sleep in on Saturday, but get up at your normal time on Sunday again. This will not only reduce SP, but will give you more alert hours for the coming week.

Making Your Bedroom a Safe Haven

To reinforce a renewed respect for sleeping, it is important to turn the bedroom into a sanctuary from the rest of the world. Having the chance to relax and get ready for sleep is just as important as securing those precious hours of quality rest.

Take a good look at your bedroom. Now, is this a room that you can relax in? A room you want to hang out in? A room that is neat and uncluttered? Lastly, do you feel safe? Can you lock the door? Bedrooms that pass this test are bedrooms that do their job. Nightmares feed on fear, and you want to feel confident in the middle of the night that you're safe.

Below are some points to consider for making your bedroom more conducive to sleep and good dreams.

Lighting

Light easily makes it through our closed eyelids, and it is the #1 factor for resetting the diurnal clock. So if you want to have quality sleep past dawn, it's important to have curtains that don't let the light shine through them. This is especially important for shift workers who sleep during the day. When bedding down, absolute darkness is best, but a small night-light won't hurt.

Lighting is important before going to sleep too. Relax with a good book in the light of a bedside lamp (with a warm full spectrum 60-watt bulb) rather than with an overhead fluorescent fixture that creates a stark and clinical environment. Indirect light from the corners of the room can be soothing, too.

Clean Linens

Likewise, you want to feel cozy crawling into bed. Change your sheets once a week; it's amazing how this simple act can improve morale. Pillows also should be replaced every two years or so; they quickly soak up allergens that can subtly affect sleep quality. Also pay attention to the laundry soap used to clean linens—there are more choices than ever at the grocery store for scented or unscented laundry soap.

Cool, Clear Air

Take a deep breath when you're next in you bedroom. Proper ventilation is important for sleep health. Even in winter, you can use an overhead fan to keep the air moving. Paradoxically, running a fan can actually lower your heating bills as it will push the warm air that has risen to the ceiling back to the floor, so you are likely to not run the heater as much. Being too hot can also bring on disturbing dreams and sleep awakenings. Most people are comfortable with slightly cool air and a good blanket rather than a hot room and a sheet. If you live in the tropics, keep the window open and allow the ventilation to work its magic.

A recent dream study indicated that bad smells can induce nightmares, and good smells can lessen disturbing dreams.[11] So besides just keeping the bedroom clean, you may want to have fresh flowers in a vase, a dish of fresh herbs, or some aromatherapy candles.

Other considerations: a hamper with a lid can keep those gym socks (and monsters under the bed) in check.

Noise Pollution

Not everyone can live somewhere that is absolutely quiet at night. For the rest of us, a fan does double duty by circulating the air, as well as creating *white noise*, which is a consistent sound that masks erratic noises. If you suffer from SP, chances are you are a light sleeper as well. There are also many white noise machines on the market, retailing between $45 - $150, with options that range from the sound of crashing waves to the sound of crickets chirping.

What Not to Have in the Bedroom

Television and Computers

Avoid having computers and TVs on in your bedroom. Even though watching TV, playing a DVD, or involving yourself in a video game before bed can be relaxing, it does more harm than good by confusing circadian rhythms with the erratic bright lights. The violent content of many movies, news programs, and video games can also lead to nightmares.[12] This is your sanctuary from the world, after all.

Work-related Stuff

If it's work related, don't let it past the threshold of your bedroom. Do your taxes, your bills, and your client work somewhere else—*anywhere* else. Segregating your sleep from your work is even more necessary if you work at home, and the boundaries between working and resting are already blurred.

Food

Keeping food in the bedroom is not recommended for several reasons. First, smelling food can trigger hunger at inappropriate times. Secondly, food can greatly increase the presence of allergy-inducing molds and mildews in the air. By the way: eating meat and cheese before bed is also linked to nightmares; nightmare researcher Ernest Hartmann calls this the "Pepperoni Pizza Effect."[13]

Before Bed Activities

I recommend giving yourself 45 minutes to unwind in your bedroom before bed. Otherwise, the sanctuary effect of the bedroom will not be optimal. We sleep more soundly and have better dreams if we relax before going to bed, rather than falling asleep with a thud after a long day of struggles. How to relax is highly personal, but here's some basic suggestions.

Reading Before Bed

Reading in bed can be relaxing and a perfect way to shut the chattering mind down. Something to consider: if you read in bed during the afternoon, you could actually be undoing the association between the bed and sleeping. So only read in bed if you intend to sleep afterwards.

Listening to Music

The easiest way to "cement" your wind-down time is to shut the door and put on some relaxing music. This also lets others in your household know that you are not to be disturbed unless in case of an emergency. Why not put on the music, light an aromatherapy candle, and settle down to your book?

Prayer

If you have a religious tradition or a spiritual practice, touching base before bed is a wonderful way to reduce stress and prepare the mind, body and soul for sleep. A "gratitude prayer" is one of the best medicines for warming the heart and relaxing the mind. List what you feel thankful for today, and dwell on that sense of gratitude. Prayer also helps with making your bedroom feel safe and connected to your highest ideals, an important consideration when SP bears down later in the dark night.

Sexuality

The bedroom, in my opinion, is for relaxing, sleeping, and for the love life. If you share a bedroom with your partner, make a rule to never start an argument the last hour before bed. Going to bed after a fight, when you are still angry, can increase your chance of a restless night, as well as the chance of nightmares.

More Tactics for Improving Sleep Hygiene

Vary Sleeping Positions

Paralysis nightmares occur most often when we sleep on our backs. We stay in light sleep longer in this position. We also experience more breathing-related problems, such as snoring and micro-awakenings.

Limit sleeping on your back, especially while falling asleep. When you wake up in the middle of the night, be sure to roll over to a new side. This is good not only for sleep health but also for eliminating cramps and body soreness upon awakening.

Take Naps

If getting enough sleep at night is impossible, take an afternoon nap. Siestas are common all over the world—except in the U.S., Britain, and Australia, which also happen to be the most sleep-deprived cultures in the world.

Turn the phone ringer off, shut the door, and put on an eye mask if need be. Eat your lunch at home and use the rest of your hour to nap. Even a fifteen minute nap can make a difference in emotional renewal and late afternoon productivity.

Regular Exercise

The brain stays healthy with regular cardiovascular activity, which is why sleep is more restful and comes more easily with active lifestyles. You don't have to go to the gym, or take a grueling run on an icy morning. Pick up a physically active hobby or an old favorite activity that you used to do or something you've always wanted to try. If you don't like it, chances are you won't do it.

Whether you choose something social or solitary, the most important thing is to get your heart rate up for about 15 to 20 minutes. Moderate exercise also helps with emotional renewal, which lessens general anxiety, as well as discharges the after-effects of a recent nightmare.

Dietary Considerations for Optimal Sleep Health

What we eat and drink has a direct effect on our sleep health, as well as the susceptibility to SP and nightmares.

Reducing Stimulants and Alcohol

Caffeine – the Elephant in the Room

Most of the world drinks coffee, cola, or black tea everyday. These beverages all contain medium to high levels of caffeine, a powerful stimulant. There's tons of research that indicates that caffeine in moderation can be healthful: it quickens the mind, suppresses uncontrollable appetites, and can even elevate sperm counts in men.

But because our culture thrives on caffeine, there is little talk about the negative effects of drinking three or more cups of coffee a day. Caffeine clearly increases anxiety, a leading cause of sleep paralysis. It increases the amount of time needed to fall sleep, as well as decreases the quality of deep sleep and REM sleep.[14]

19

Long story short: By reducing your coffee, tea, chocolate, and cola intake, you will immediately begin getting more restful sleep. The secret is moderation and timing. Because of caffeine's effect on our wakefulness cycle, it's best to limit caffeinated beverages to the morning and early afternoon. The same is true with all other stimulants.

Beer and Alcohol – Putting a cap on nightcaps

Alcohol is a perplexing substance. Millions of people have discovered that a nightcap can put them to sleep quickly, but research suggests that alcohol actually contributes to insomnia in the long run.[15] More directly, alcohol suppresses REM (dreaming) sleep, which then causes a REM rebound effect towards the end of the night.[16] These REM rebound dreams are often SP nightmares because the REM transition is not smooth, so the conscious mind is more often made aware of the process of muscle paralysis that accompanies REM.

That said, beer has another ingredient that is actually a reliable sleep aid: hops. Hops is an aromatic herb that has been added to beers for hundreds of years. If you have to have a nightcap, have a cup of beer, not a shot of whisky. The typical beer (a lager or pilsner ale) is full of carbohydrates, a dash of hops, and just enough alcohol to act as a sedative.[17] For more of the hops effect, go for an India Pale Ale or a California style ale.

My advice: Every once in a while a nightcap is okay, but don't do it habitually. In general, don't drink a few hours before bed. The Mayans of Central America, who are known for their fully developed philosophy of dreams, say that drinking alcohol after noon is a sure way to block good dreams and invite restlessness.[18]

Changing your habits for these two substances (caffeine and alcohol) will have an almost instantaneous effect of lessening SP nightmares. Moderation and timing is the key to having a productive day and a restful night.

Sleepytime Foods and Supplements

Some foods are good for restful nights because they have high concentrations of vitamins and supplements that promote healthy brain chemistry. Add these foods to a well-balanced dinner or a light snack an hour before bedtime.

Tryptophan

Tryptophan is an amino acid that is most commonly associated with turkey dinners. "The thanksgiving effect" is well known in the United States as a necessary nap on the couch after eating a harvest feast. This amino acid is a building block for several key brain chemicals that regulate the sleep cycle, including melatonin and serotonin.

But tryptophan is actually in dozens of common foods besides turkey. Fruits and vegetables with high levels of tryptophan include: bananas, mangoes, dried dates, chickpeas, sunflower seeds, pumpkin seeds, peanuts, potatoes, kale, yams, and watermelon. Tryptophan-rich grains include oats and wheat. Spaghetti is a great source that doubles as a comfort food. Other animal products with lots of tryptophan include red meat, chicken, lamb, eggs, fish, milk, and yogurt—as well as cheddar, Parmesan, and cottage cheese.[19]

Melatonin

Melatonin is a naturally occurring compound that is an effective sleep aid. In higher doses, however, it can increase dream bizarreness, which can be counterproductive if you are trying to stay away from nightmares. It's available as a natural supplement, but for low doses, stick to the natural sources like nuts and herbs.

Seeds with high melatonin include white mustard, black mustard, wolfberry, fenugreek seed, sunflower, fennel, and alfalfa. Sprinkle some of these in a salad or blend them into some yogurt for a nutritious midnight snack.

Herbs with melatonin include Huang-qin, St John's wort, and Feverfew. All three of these can have four micrograms of melatonin per gram of the herb. These natural sources contain only a thousandth of the amount contained in melatonin pills, so it's a safe way to experiment with its soothing effects.

Drink Herbal Teas

You don't have to look hard to find herbal teas that act as gentle and natural sleep aids. Chamomile, rose hips, and mint are my favorites. Find a tea sweetened with licorice root, too, to help it go down without adding sugar to your system. These teas aid in digestion and also soothe the mind. They also can replace the habit of eating ice cream or having a tonic before bed.

Other Herbs for Relaxing

Any herb that reduces stress and aids in relaxation can be used in a tea, as a tincture, or placed in a dream pillow. Some herbs that naturopaths and herbalists recognize include mugwort, skullcap, California poppy, ginger, mint, and Gingko.

Known Pharmaceuticals that Affect Paralysis Nightmares

Certain pharmaceuticals can help prevent paralysis nightmares, and others can aggravate the condition. In general, stimulants will increase SP, and antidepressants will decrease the symptoms.

Some antidepressants work by increasing serotonin levels, which also decrease REM sleep. Serotonin re-uptake inhibitors (SSRIs) that contain fluoxetine can drastically reduce paralysis nightmares, but often at the expense of dreaming in general[20]. Monoamine oxidase inhibitors (MAOIs) and tricyclic antidepressants also have a nightmare-dampening effect.[21]

The same is true of anticholinergics, such as ipratropium, a type of bronchodilator used to treat lung obstruction diseases like chronic bronchitis, emphysema, and asthma.

And interestingly enough, Pausinystalia yohimbe, a readily available herbal supplement, may also decrease SP symptoms.

A word of caution: yohimbe contains yohimbine, a powerful psychoactive substance, and has a potential for overdose. Yohimbe also has been used to treat sexual dysfunction and Post-Traumatic Stress Disorder.[22]

ADHD medication, on the other hand, has been linked to increased levels of paralysis nightmares. Sometimes, not taking the pills near bedtime can make a positive difference.[23]

Note that I do not recommend that someone stop taking medication (or begin taking medication that has not been prescribed to them). The pharmaceutical treatments of isolated sleep paralysis and recurrent isolated sleep paralysis are not in opposition to the self-help tactics employed in this book. Rather, consider this information as a point of departure in discussions with your medical provider.

CHAPTER THREE
Feeling Safe Again

Paralysis nightmares and hypnagogic hallucinations are not just a physical malady that "happens" to us. We are not passive victims. While the mind-state is triggered by physical conditions, the experience that follows is shaped by our thoughts and fears. If we don't feel safe in our own home, we may invite more nightmares. And when the nightmares recur several times in a night, we may feel frazzled and end up staying up all night—afraid to go back to bed—and end up in a cycle of insomnia and REM rebound. We may even begin to question our sanity.

However, you don't necessarily need to see a psychiatrist to get over these nightmares. And, armed with the practices in this chapter, you will soon be able to fall asleep easily again. The truth is that each of us has the ability to meet the fear that arises when we come face to face with the unknown. As psychologist and dream expert Scott Sparrow told me, what we often find in the unknown is not death (as we feared) but a chance to live more fully.

This innate ability is the subject of this chapter: how to lower your stress, confront fear, and feel safe again. But first, let's put the nightmares in perspective. Here is some background on the psychological aspects of iSP.

Personality Characteristics of Life-Long Sufferers

Not much is known about family patterns with regards to SP and hypnagogic hallucinations (HH), although many psychiatrists believe it has a hereditary component. Lifelong experiencers of SP also have certain traits in common. These associations[24] are still speculative and incomplete, but they parallel results from studies of nightmare sufferers.

Some personality traits of SP experiencers include having:
- A creative or artistic drive
- An increased sensitivity to social tension and other people's pain and suffering
- A tendency towards social anxiety
- A fantasy-prone temperament, including engaging in daydreaming and other deep imaginative activities for long periods of time
- The ability to be easily hypnotized
- An increased likelihood to suffer from depression or a panic disorder
- An increased likelihood to report psychic or other unusual experiences

Women have SP more than men, and African-American women in particular have elevated rates of SP/HH, perhaps correlated with higher rates of anxiety disorders.[25]

Some famous SP sufferers include US President Woodrow Wilson and surrealist artist Salvador Dali. Because sleep paralysis is featured in Melville's *Moby Dick*, as well as Edgar Allan Poe's short story "The Black Cat," chances are these literary giants also encountered SP.

Separating the Components of the Experience

It's important to separate sleep paralysis from hypnagogic

hallucinations (HH) because understanding these components will help you gain familiarity and mastery of this fascinating mental state.

1. The physical sensation of paralysis. You can't move. You can't scream. You can't do anything as the feeling of weight presses down on your chest and throat.

2. Next, there is a conscious reaction of fear, dread, and terror as your sense of helplessness escalates. For some, the fear of being attacked is so intense it is called "death anxiety."[26]

3. The scariest part of all—HH visions which can be visual, auditory, tactile, and even odoriferous. HH includes the hooded apparition who shows up on the side of the bed or the invisible presence who lays a cold hand on your helpless body. Also spiders, insects, and other creatures like scurrying and nibbling rats.

Together, these symptoms of SP/HH can reinforce each other by our participation, whether the reaction is fear, anticipation, objective curiosity, or passionate surrender. What we bring to these encounters helps determine the outcome because dreaming is a co-creative mental act, not a given.[27] The path is not set: we are surrounded by choices and possibilities in every moment.

The Expectation Effect

Psychologically, what happens when fear spirals into a nightmare is a feedback loop known as the *expectation effect*. Fear caused by the paralysis leads us to bring up past experiences that are similar to this sensation. Often, these are experiences or stories of being oppressed by another person, of being held down, and especially for women, of being sexually violated. In a world where 1 out of 6 women will be sexually assaulted in their lifetimes, these fears are all too common.[28]

Once the subconscious connections have been made between the present sensations and memories or fears, the brain begins to interpret the experience according to these narratives. If the paralysis is followed by hypnagogic hallucinations (HH), then these visions will typically include a sinister agent who wants to do us harm. We end up manifesting our worst nightmare without realizing it.

Sleep Paralysis and Inner Crisis

If you have never experienced iSP before and are suddenly having multiple encounters a night, something other than diet and sleep habits may be involved. In some cases, SP may be a symptom of a larger crisis that involves your sense of meaning, faith, or spirituality. Conversely, if you are exploring lucid dreaming for the first time, disturbing paralysis nightmares may come with the package. In both cases, it is appropriate to look at your deepest beliefs in order to ward off the manifestation of your worst fears.

The greatest ally here is the power of our *core beliefs*. This is the sense of order and balance we have about how the world works. Even if you are not religious or even spiritually minded, you still have a belief system that operates daily, guiding your thoughts and actions, and governing your sense of justice. It may be the belief that God is Love, or it could be a reliance on rationalism and the power of the scientific mind. The key is to tap into these core beliefs and lean against them in times of need.

The reason this is so important is that the hypnagogic visions that follow paralysis *are already working on this deep level*, but they can work against us. They are tapping into the negative side of our beliefs when we experience fear. These fears manifest as our personal visions of chaos, death, and true evil. The worst things, in other words. That's why psychologists list paralysis nightmares as one possible indication of a *spiritual emergency*.[29]

This is no new-age mumbo jumbo: Spiritual emergency is a

psychological condition that is listed in the DSM IV[30], the latest edition of the diagnostic manual for the American Psychiatric Association. Also called "religious or spiritual problems," spiritual emergency is often characterized by disturbing visions and experiences that can be linked to a serious crisis about the meaning of life and existence. The crisis often happens at times of transition into adulthood, into parenthood, and into mid-life, for example.[31] They also come with the ingestion of psychedelic drugs or participation in a group ritual.

Because paralysis nightmares are often cited as one symptom of a spiritual emergency, the question to ask is, "Why am I having these experiences *now*, at this time of my life?"

Seen in this light, SP can serve as a metaphor for the fact that our old defenses are no longer functioning as well as before. It's also an indicator that life stress is becoming overwhelming or that we are having trouble coping with major life changes, such as a death in the family or trouble on the job front. When this stress manifests as SP, the body is paralyzed, the mind is in fight or flight, and there's nowhere to run.

So, instead, we must take a stand. For some, this looks like courage. For others, it is faith. I cannot speak for you, and I certainly am not advocating a particular religion or spiritual viewpoint in this book. That said, if you can tread in these deep waters, you will learn how to turn the fear on its side and break free of these disturbing nightmares.

What follows are some practices that are effective in breaking down the psychological precursors to SP. These are behavioral changes and habits that, with a little practice, will influence the mind and body to take back the night.

Getting Grounded

Here are some ways to reconnect with core beliefs, reduce stress, and encourage feelings of safety in the world.

Discontinue Intense Mental/Bodily Practices

This may seem counterintuitive, but temporarily reducing intense mental and bodily practices (such as concentrative meditation, Hatha yoga or chanting practices) during repetitive SP attacks will help you to normalize. These practices can be mentally and emotionally destabilizing and further exasperate the situation.[32] On the other hand, relaxation practices, such as regular breathing meditations and mild forms of yoga that do not build heat, can be helpful.

Eat more heavy foods

Another excellent grounding technique is adding more whole grains, meat, and dairy to your diet. As discussed in Chapter 2, a small carb-heavy snack before bed can also help with getting to sleep. On the other hand, reduce sugar and caffeine, as well as cannabis and alcohol.

Pick up a Relaxing Hobby

Spend some time each day doing a simple and relaxing physical activity. This could be gardening or knitting, swimming or taking a leisurely walk each afternoon. Hobbies that require relaxed focus are often found in the dusty attic of our youth. It's a great excuse for picking up the coin collection or putting together a model car.

Express Yourself

Drawing, painting, dancing, writing, or playing a musical instrument are satisfying ways to express what you are going through. This kind of artistic translation can provide some distance from the nightmares and fears of going to sleep. I have personally found journaling to be one of the most relaxing and grounding activities in my life. One of my morning routines is to journal my dreams. This also has an emotional effect; it provides psychological distance from the encounters.

Sometimes You Can Go Back

Sufferers of nightmares naturally bring up questions about the divine after a terrifying encounter with SP, especially if fear elevates into death anxiety. In particular, the religion we had as children can come to our rescue when facing moments of pure panic and terror.

It can be surprising when these religious feelings resurface. For instance, I remember once crying out during an episode of SP, "I trust in God!" Later, I felt embarrassed by my outburst because I had not thought about my spirituality in those terms for at least twenty years. But I have since discovered that such experiences are commonplace. Indeed, in times of stress, we look for guidance, and there may be no clearer path than in reclaiming the spiritual faith of an earlier time. In the dream, this is doubly-so, as dreaming is a state of consciousness that highlights long-term memories and emotional responses. In other words, we are neurologically primed for the resurfacing of deep memories in the dream, including our long-forgotten childhood experiences of faith, our envisioning of the divine, and philosophical concerns about death that were raised but never answered in youth.

This can also be an opportune time for contemplating your faith-of-origin in a new light, as these nightmares tend to be repetitive and take place over a number of weeks. What remains true for you, and what can you let go? By spending a little time pondering this question, you may find that your childhood belief system is still intact, despite any bitterness that has lodged here in the decades since. During this process, you may also challenge a deeply held belief or myth about yourself that is no longer true. Tending to this source by clearing out the tired myths and investing in the ones that still hold true is a process well worth the trouble.

Part II:
Confronting the Apparition

CHAPTER FOUR
Getting To Know The Stranger

The apparition encounter is one of the least understood and scariest aspects of SP nightmares. These realistic visions are hypnagogic hallucinations (HH) and include feeling a presence, seeing someone/something in your bedroom, and being assaulted by a horrible creature. According to medical anthropologist David Hufford, apparition experiences occur in about 14-18% of isolated sleep paralysis cases. These encounters are among the most terrifying visions that people have ever reported,[33] and these are the dreams that keep us awake at night, afraid of going back to sleep. Sometimes, it's just a feeling that someone is in the room watching us. On other occasions, we may actually feel someone (or something) sitting down on the bed next to us. Finally, some people are touched or even abused by an apparition who holds them down, chokes them, and may even sexually abuse them. Terror is not too strong a word to use here because it seems as if nothing can be done.

Something can be done. Even though we are paralyzed during this hypnagogic hallucination (HH), we still have the ability to control our fear. There are also several windows of opportunity to influence what happens when the Stranger appears at your bedside.

But first, let's review some theories about how the apparitions manifest in the mind and the cultural significance of these encounters around the world.

Psychological Theories about SP Entities

The Threat Vigilance System

Scientists have had little to say about these apparition visions until recently. Current cognitive psychology research suggests that SP with HH triggers a threat-awareness scan in the brain known as the vigilance system.[34] This process is largely unconscious and normally is responsible for identifying possible threats ("What's that noise?") and making quick decisions about our physical safety ("Oh, it's just the cat."). But in SP/HH, our eyes may be open, but we are projecting our dreams into physical space. The combination of sensing and imagining makes the system go a little haywire, causing the vigilance system to stay activated because it cannot clarify exactly what the threat is. "Threat!" the system calls, again and again. This, in turn, makes our fear intensify because a part of the brain responsible for intense emotions, the amygdala, is already heightened in this dream state.[35] So we project images of our worst fears into the room, intensifying our fear even further as the Stranger takes form.

It is an escalating fear-vision feedback system that precipitates the apparition beside our bed with its darkened face and evil-feeling presence. We co-create the nightmare without even knowing it.

In my mind, this physical explanation is incomplete because it doesn't explain why the triggered vigilance system interprets the vague dream forms as a human-like presence. Why not a tidal wave, an earthquake, or an avalanche? After all, these are common themes in many other kinds of nightmares. A caveat: some people who have HH without sleep paralysis (muscle atonia) often see other kinds of imagery, especially bugs and creepy-crawlies. The difference between HH with SP and HH without is not understood, but most likely has to do with the perceived physical threat instigated by the SP muscle atonia.

Neurotheology and Spirits

This is where the research of anthropologist Michael Winkelman comes in handy. Winkelman suggests that humans are hard-wired to see spirits; it's part of our genetic make-up. Known as *neurotheology*[36], this view posits that the universality of seeing spirits does not necessarily mean that "spirits are real," but certainly that the experiences are authentic, and not just made up by a combination of wishful thinking and cultural loading from myths and fairy tales.

Further, Winkelman suggests that we are predisposed to see human-like spirits because our minds are accustomed to perceiving the world as having qualities like ourselves. When something sudden happens—a peal of thunder—our first question is, "Who did that?" So in times of ambiguity, projecting a human-like actor into the scene is our first cognitive line of defense. Why? Maybe because you can try to reason with a Thunder God, but not with nature herself. This has appeal from an evolutionary perspective because the greatest danger to a human life has never been the tiger or the lion, but social ostracization and abandonment.

Neurotheology brings a crucial insight into the worldwide perception of the Stranger apparition: in times of distress, we tend to perceive self-like entities in the world.

Dreams, Archetypes, and Entities

Dreams also bring us closer to the unconscious frameworks with which we see the world. REM dreaming is, neurologically speaking, a visionary state of mind. Activation of the limbic system brings strong emotions, combined with an enhanced access to long-term memory—and a depression of short-term memory so we don't tend to question who or where we are.[37] Add the intense firing of the parts of the brain that bring mental imagery, and you have dreaming: a potent mix of visual-emotional metaphors that link to our deepest memories and experiences.

This neurological basis of SP visions in REM sleep provides additional support for the archetypal psychology of Carl Jung and James Hillman.[38] These depth psychologies address the issue of visitors in dream visions as communication between conscious mind and unconscious processes. These processes are autonomous, occurring on their own accord, whether or not we pay attention to them. However, directing heightened awareness towards these images can quicken the mind's digestion and integration of these ancient impulses, personal myths, and cultural and familial expectations. Some of the archetypal images that may arise from these deep psychological processes are human figures, such as the wise old man and wise woman, and the inner child.

The Shadow

One of Jung and Hillman's insights into our propensity to create nightmarish figures in dreams and visions is that sometimes we are faced with confrontational images that just will not go away. This is the archetype of the Shadow. Poet Robert Bly describes the shadow everything we don't want to look at that we threw into a bag long ago.[39] While the shadow can be parts of ourselves that we have disowned (such as greed, weakness, or an undeveloped artistic ability), it can also be something about our culture, our nation's history, or our socio-economic class that we don't like to think about. The shadow could express poverty, racism, or a landscape that has been repeatedly stripped of its natural habitats. These unconscious patterns can play out over and over throughout history, as well as in our dreams.[40] In SP visions, sometimes the apparition comes not just to be scary, but to be heard.

Still, we want to be careful not to reduce the apparitions to a symbol or concept. Each meeting is unique, alive, and dynamic. I can tell you from personal experience that the Stranger, or any dream figure, doesn't take kindly to being called a "representation." Would you?

Psychic Dimensions of SP Apparitions

The literature on the connection between hypnagogic hallucinations and psychic effects is pretty vast and comes from many parallel threads. Telepathy, ESP, and mutual dreams have been cited in religious texts and accounts, 19th century spiritualism and occult texts, and in modern controlled studies. In general, dream researchers who look at this aspect of dreaming suggest that hypnagogia (and its sister state in sleep awakening, hypnopompia) seem to be "more conducive to telepathy," as Simon Sherwood reports in his 2002 meta-analysis.[41]

Neurology, of course, does not really provide much support on this topic, except to say that HH are more similar in brain activation to trance states than ordinary dreaming.[42] Heightened alpha brain waves are reported in SP/HH,[43] just as with OBEs and some forms of deep meditation, all of which are correlated with psi accounts. Field anthropologists who study indigenous peoples have also reported numerous anomalous psi events, usually saving their declaration for after they secure tenure or retire.[44] These events, while hard to replicate in a lab, become an accepted part of life for those who are open to uncanny and bizarre experiences, such as synchronicity and precognitive dreams.

Just as telekinesis effects are weaker in the laboratory than reported in their natural setting (such as poltergeist accounts in old homes and other historic locations), sleep paralysis encounters that occur in the lab also rarely have psychic or uncanny dimensions to them. Rather than dismiss all these accounts as fanciful, especially those that include mutual (shared) sleep paralysis encounters, it is more reasonable to assume that something more than our western atomistic psychology is at work here. We need more experienced sleep paralysis visionaries in the field, dreaming at sacred sites and historical locations where these events are prominent. More techniques of this nature are listed in Part III.

Sleep Paralysis and Place: A Geologic Hypothesis

Psychologist Jorge Conesa-Sevilla has put forward an ecopsychological hypothesis about SP/HH. Ecopsychology is the study of the mind in association with the natural environment. Conesa-Sevilla suggests that the uncanny state of mind may be triggered by geological anomalies and points out that cultures living in the "Ring of Fire," the geomagnetically unstable areas of Central America, the Pacific Coast of the US, Southern Alaska, Hawaii, and Indonesia, have a much more developed vocabulary for sleep paralysis and its accompanying hallucinations than anywhere else in the world. [45] Many of the indigenous peoples of these territories are dreaming cultures that pay attention to, and actively invite, the dreaming arts, such as lucid dreaming, reverie, and trance states.[46] Given that geomagnetic effects have been shown to alter consciousness, Conesa-Sevilla's hypothesis is not so unlikely.

Similarly, archaeologist Paul Devereux has noted that SP is one state of consciousness among many that transgress the normal boundaries of mental imagery (without straying into psychosis) and may be responsible for some mental events interpreted as hauntings.[47] In both of these theories, then, the Stranger can be seen as emerging from local environmental conditions, as well as from the dreamer's own mind and cultural upbringing.

The Stranger Interpreted Through History

The phenomenon of the Stranger has occurred throughout recorded history and around the world. This spirit with a thousand faces[48] has a long distinguished history of being the scariest thing around. Many things that go bump in the night could take place during SP nightmares. Here are some examples from history books:

Ghosts and Hauntings

Many tales of hauntings in Europe and the US take place when the witness is lying in bed awake and suddenly feels a presence in the room. At the same time, he or she notices the onset of paralysis. In many of these classic accounts, an apparition may come into the room, sit on the bed, or start choking the witness with ghostly hands. Other accounts mention fighting with ghosts or specters and finally "pushing" them off.

Scrooge's encounter with the ghost of Marley in Charles Dickens' *Christmas Carol* is a good example, as this fictional narrative has many SP features, such as feeling a presence in the room, followed by the sound of chains and approaching footsteps, and the narrator's adamant conclusion that he is awake despite the otherworldly nature of the encounter. Individuals not accustomed to lucid dreaming, iSP, and other extraordinary states do not understand that you can be hallucinating while still in your "right mind," leading them prematurely to supernatural explanations.[49] Rather, I suggest that our concept of material reality is incomplete.

Witchcraft and Demons

In Europe and the US, belief in witchcraft has a long history. According to 17th century American court documents, for example, a woman was tried as a witch because her accuser said that her apparition came into his room at night and climbed on top of him. This was called "witch riding" and still is in some African-American communities.[50]

In medieval Europe, accounts suggest that demons could sit on the sufferer's chest and sexually molest them against their will. These demons were known as the Incubus (male) and the Succubus (female).[51] The *Malleus Maleficarum* ("the Witch's Hammer"), a guidebook written in 1486 and used to prosecute pagans and witches during the Inquisition, suggests that witches are those who voluntarily submit themselves (and have intercourse) with the Incubus demons. Some succubi legends suggest female demons collected men's sperm during forced intercourse at night.

Fairies and Little People

The fairy folklore of the British Isles is often framed around an abduction story. The fairy gives the victim a drink or otherwise induces paralysis and then absconds with the victim to fairyland, always returning him safely to his bed.[52] In some fairy tales, however, children are stolen and never returned.[53] Incidentally, fairies were also blamed for paralysis in livestock, which was called "fairy-riding."

In Norse mythology, black elves known as *Svartálfar* were feared because of their paralyzing arrows, called elf shot. These dwarf-like creatures were known for sitting on the sleeper's chest and whispering horrible things into the dreamer's ear. In German, the word for nightmare, *"Albtraum"* still translates to "elf dream." Sleep paralysis entities seem to consist more of the earth fairies, such as trolls, dwarves, and wood nymphs, as opposed to the more delicate winged fairies and water pixies. In the Germanic tradition, Kobolds or Brownies were associated with poltergeist activity— basically acting as trickster figures in the household; they were blamed with moving objects and causing mischief.

The Sidhe of Ireland

In Irish mythology, the Sidhe are the spirits of the Tuatha de Danann, the ancient peoples of Ireland. These fairies progress along "fairy ways" or roads of historical significance. Dreamers in Ireland sometimes hear the *Sidhe* at night, marching down the path in a royal procession. This tradition is reminiscent of the Hawaiian Night Marchers described in the next section.

Vampires

This passage from Bram Stoker's *Dracula* speaks for itself:

> There was in the room the same thin white mist that I had before discovered . . . I felt the same vague terror which had come to me before and the same sense of some presence . . . Then indeed, my heart sank within me: Beside the bed, as if it had stepped out of the mist—or rather as if the mist had turned into his figure, for it had completely disappeared— stood a tall, thin man, all in black. I knew him at once from the description of the others. The waxen face; the high aquiline nose, on which the light fell in a thin white line; the parted red lips, with the sharp white teeth showing between; and the red eyes . . . I would have screamed out, only that I was paralyzed.[54]

Sound familiar? The detail about the mist transforming into the dark figure is a clue that we'll come back to soon.

The Stranger Across Cultures

Sleep paralysis is recognized all over the world, and the HH apparition is usually the central defining feature of the experience. We have the work of folklorist and medical anthropologist David Hufford to thank for first recognizing the validity of SP/HH experiences. Many assumed these accounts were "just cultural stories," but they may, in turn, be the experiential backbone to the Boogyman himself. In Japan, the Stranger is called "Kanashibari," and many believe the figure is a retaliating spirit or ancestor. In Thailand, the nightmares are known as "Phi um," which means "being enveloped by a ghost." In Newfoundland, people whisper about the old hag syndrome, and in Hong Kong, ghost oppression.[55]

Meanwhile, Hawaii is haunted by "night marchers," the Hauka'I po, who are respected warriors from the ancient days. The sound of their footsteps and pounding drums as they walk is fearful because of the belief that looking into the eyes of the warriors will bring death. What makes this variation interesting is the focus on the auditory hallucination of the marching feet and drums.

In the Inuit cultures of the far North, SP/HH is interpreted as an attack by a shaman or some malevolent demon. It is also possible in this same state to travel to the land of the dead. Youth in the same culture, however, are more likely to attribute SP/HH to the Christian notion of the "devil trying to get you."[56]

Refugees seem to suffer terribly from SP/HH, as the phenomenon is associated with panic disorder and Post-traumatic stress disorder. In Cambodia, SP/HH is translated as "the ghost pushes you down."[57] In several of these chilling accounts, the apparition takes the shape of individuals who were murdered during the brutal Khmer Rouge regime. Another terrifying example from this culture, documented by J.A. Cheyne in 2001, is a trio of humanoid creatures covered with fur and with long fangs that leer over the bed. Among Cambodian refugees in the U.S., the SP/HH encounter is culturally linked to the Sudden Unexpected

Nocturnal Death Syndrome (SUNDS), a mysterious pattern of deaths in healthy adults that now appears to be an inherited heart disorder known elsewhere as Brugada syndrome.[58] But the folkloric tie to the nightmare is strong. In essence, the Hmong of Cambodia, Laos, Thailand, and Vietnam, consider SP/HH an unsuccessful attempt by a demon to kill the dreamer. The fear of this encounter naturally elevates the fear during SP, resulting in intense death anxiety. However, there is no evidence that sleep paralysis is a contributing cause of death of SUNDS or Brugada syndrome. Still, some researchers note that the fear of supernatural assault is so great among the Hmong that sleep paralysis may itself be a cause of Post-traumatic stress disorder (PTSD).[59]

Cheyne also describes an SP account of a Native American woman whose apparition takes the shape of her childhood myths: "Spider woman came from the ceiling and wrapped me up and sang songs to me. It was then and later when the Deerwoman would come and stand at the foot of my bed."[60] Although still frightening, Spider woman and Deerwoman are a part of her religious tradition.

The evidence of the Stranger in so many cultures today, as well as throughout history, indicates that people have been coping with this unique vision for a long time. The important thing is to know how to deal with the apparition when it calls.

Despite all cultural differences, the components of the Stranger's visit are common around the world. Understanding the progression can give us a glimpse of the best times to alter the course of the imagery so the encounter happens on your terms. Keep in mind that these generalizations are preliminary. The vision does not have to go through all of the following stages in this order, or any at all.

Mapping the Apparition

Four Stages of the Stranger
1. *Presence*
   At first, you only feel the "presence" of someone else in the

room or perhaps at the doorway. The sense of presence is not based on any visual imagery but is rather a "gut feeling" that you are no longer alone. This is usually an uncomfortable feeling because, of course, you cannot move or talk. Because of fear, it's common to think that this "other person" is evil. Some people also feel that the presence is watching them.

2. Shadowy form

Next, the Stranger will make itself known, but it is hard to see or ambiguous in nature. You may feel as if someone cruel is standing right behind your head or just out-of-view. Here you may actually see a darkened figure in the doorway or a silhouette by the window. But you cannot see the figure's face. Sometimes, like in the Dracula story above, there may be mists or fog that coalesce into a dark figure. What makes this stage of the Stranger so terrifying is precisely its unknown identity. As we'll see soon, this is also the stage when you can most easily break out of the Stranger's grasp.

3. Intruder

Sometimes, after feeling the Presence, you may then sense that the Stranger is getting closer to you. You may feel the mattress sink as he or she sits next to you on the bed. Or you may just sense that the Stranger is standing right next to you. Also, some people report hearing the Stranger's footsteps approaching. Often, the sound is like someone shuffling his feet. This sound is also heard during the first stage of Presence. Others hear the sound of something being dragged across the floor, like a heavy clothes bag or even chains (such as the Ghost of Marley). Bad odors are frequently reported, which is striking as most dreams do not include this sense impression. Finally, you may get a glimpse of what the figure looks like from a distance. At this stage, fear can be so intense that the sound of your throbbing heartbeat may be louder than anything else. Many people who have remained quiet, hoping the Stranger would go away, start to scream—only to find out that they can't.

What does the apparition look like? The visage is different for everyone, but suffice to say that it parallels your worst fears. And there may be more than one Stranger. Indeed, some people seem predisposed to be visited by groups of apparitions rather than a single figure. Accounts from past sufferers include descriptions of demons, hairy monsters, disfigured people, hooded figures with gleaming red or yellow eyes, the Devil, witches, hags, vampires or werewolves, giants, undead zombies, aliens with big grey eyes, and, for some, people who once tortured or sexually abused them. These figures also seem intelligent; there is a quality in their eyes that they know exactly what they are doing.

4. Incubus

In this final stage, the Stranger can make physical contact. It may put its hands on your throat, or sit on your chest and smile wickedly. Other accounts are quite graphic and disturbing. Some report sexual assault, although the threat of assault is more common. Keep in mind, an Incubus attack is *psychologically* real, and the terror it causes can actually retrigger old traumatic memories. This is why SP is taken seriously by psychologists, especially if SP is combined with other issues, such as panic disorder and PTSD.

No doubt, this encounter can take you into a terrifying dream journey. However, it does not feel like a dream. You may feel scared, but also highly alert and awake with all your thinking faculties intact. People report, "I was awake!" In this conscious nightmare, the accounts of the Stranger include continued torture, as well as travel to distant and bizarre lands. Many psychologists believe that some alien abduction memories occur during this "in between" state of awareness. When this is happening, we are in a natural visionary state lying in bed, safe and sound.

Facing the Unknown

Knowing the four major manifestations of the Stranger[61] (Presence, Shadow, Intruder, and Incubus) is the key to preventing a full-blown Incubus attack. When the Stranger is transitioning into another form, we have a special opportunity to guide the experience using the power of will and the grace of acceptance.

Let me review. Recall how the Stranger manifests because of

a hiccup of our mind's threat detection system. The ambiguity of the presence (which is a dream intruding into the waking world) triggers our fight-or-flight responses. This fear then colors the dream-like imagery that we are generating in this waking vision and solidifies the autonomous presence into a nightmare tailor-made from our personal fears and cultural background. But if you can control your fear, you can shift this encounter away from the default nightmarish progression of the Stranger, so that the fuller range of possibilities emerges.

Use the Stages of the Stranger to Gain Self-Mastery

At each stage of the Stranger's transformation, you can engage in specific mental practices to control your fear and influence what happens next.

Presence and the Shadows – At these initial stages the most important thing is to control your fear. When you sense someone in the room while in paralysis, remind yourself "This is SP and I am not in danger." Focus on your breath: breathe fully and at a moderate pace, and relax. You may also try one of the exercises described in Chapter 1 to wake up. Struggling will only increase fear and quicken the apparition's manifestation to the next stages. If you are religious, a prayer that comforts you could be recited as well. One person told me he sometimes sings a song that cheers him up.

Intruder – If you begin having hallucinations (visual signs or strange noises close to you), it's time to try a new meditation. I recommend focusing on someone you love and trust deeply. Imagine a circle of love and acceptance around you while still noticing your breath. This method dissolves the fear that drives the Intruder's creation in the mind. Sounds cheesy, but it's effective. If you are religious or spiritual, of course, focusing on God's love for you or your respect for an esteemed religious figure is valuable. You can also try to communicate with the Intruder, if you choose, that you are open to discussion. And don't forget to do the toe wiggle if

47

the experience becomes too overwhelming.

Incubus – If the Stranger has made physical contact and/or has fully emerged as a threatening figure, I recommend a more active and courageous path. It's important at this point to ask the stranger what he or she wants. Even better, ask how you can help. If you can't speak and are still paralyzed, say the words with your mind, and you may discover that you can communicate with the figure in this way. Be inquisitive and accepting, not demanding and haughty. Listen to what the figure may have to say. Sometimes, she will bend down and whisper a message, so listen carefully and with respect. Remind yourself again that you are not in danger. In some instances, this change in emotions (from fear to acceptance) can result in awakening. At other times, it can result in the Stranger shifting appearance to someone less threatening.

The Full Spectrum

Once fear is under control, the full spectrum of the SP apparition becomes known, like the opening of a secret door into a vast and bizarre, yet somehow still familiar, world. Jorge Conesa-Sevilla writes:

> I have wrestled with several hairy beings in my own bedroom for nights at a time; been visited by many hags and beauties, been whispered to, shouted at, buzzed, electrified, boomed, and hurt; been touched, pinched, and caressed by phantoms unseen; cried empty screams without anyone hearing them; been assisted by friendly entities who taught me how to move from the paralysis into lucid dreams; meditated in lucid dreams, attaining sublime bliss; been visited by angels; had countless conversations with "elders" who themselves prescribed acts that led to my being a healthier and stronger person; cavorted with, been transformed into and played with mostly mountain lions, birds

and deer; and "flown" to places indescribable until flight itself is assumed to be an intrinsic right and property of the body-mind.[62]

Conesa-Sevilla's account is inspiring. Allow me to emphasize that controlling fear does not transform all entities into positive figures like some kind of spiritual laundry mat. Rather, this practice helps account for expectation, so that the entity, "the autonomous other," can be seen with a clear mind and open heart. For example, in my SP visions and lucid dreams, I am sometimes confronted with terribly disfigured people or despicable-looking creatures. My challenge in these scenarios is to accept them and be empathetic but not pitying. If I can find this state of inner calm and acceptance of "the worst things" or the despised[63], they sometimes transform to younger and healthier entities.

At other times, my task seems to be to view the suffering of others and acknowledge their pain. "I see you and recognize your suffering" is what I say in these cases. After an interminable period, I naturally wake up with my heart open rather than in fear for my life.

Below is an example of one of my SP visions. This encounter happened five years ago and was one of the first times I was able to shift my SP away from a nightmare and into a healing process.

I know I am in sleep paralysis. I am conscious of my sleeping body on the bed, lying on my stomach. There is a woman in front of me with dark curly hair. I feel her presence first – then she steps into the room. I feel her standing beside the bed, then sitting besides me. I cannot see her face. I am scared, but I decide to trust the woman. She then sits on my lower back – I can feel her weight. Then "gravity" rotates 180 degrees so it seems like I'm now lying on my back. I feel the woman's hands on my chest area, and my whole chest becomes warm and tingly. I know she is healing me somehow, and I relax further into the sensation of being cared for. The heat extends through my body to my back, not just on the surface of my skin, a warm and deep glow.

The turning point in this experience is when I decide to trust the woman in front of me. Note how the feeling of SP is still occurring when the dream woman sits on my back. After the woman makes contact, I decide again to relax and to trust her. The encounter begins to feel healing, and I wake up refreshed.

The encounter with the Stranger is still one of the biggest mysteries in dream science. But countless people have learned how to master their fear and control their breath in order to transform their SP visions. Once you can do this, many new doors are opened.

CHAPTER FIVE
Allies, Angels, And Aliens

In Chapter 4, the terrorizing Stranger is demystified as a visionary figure amplified by fear and distrust. However, this does not mean that is all it can be. When positive feelings of love, acceptance, and trust are focused upon these apparitions, they can transform into comforting presences that are literally the stuff of legend. At other times, the apparition may keep its original form, but become more communicative and less threatening when *we* become more accessible. Nature reflects the face turned towards it.

Rather than menacing black dogs, you may find your loved childhood pet. Instead of a creepy old hag, you may receive advice from a venerable wise woman. Succubi give way to pixies and aliens to angels. This chapter reviews some of the classic manifestations that occur when we swallow our fears.

Visitations of the Dead

Of all the non-threatening iSP encounters, seeing and talking with a deceased person is one of the most common. The figure may sit on the side of the bed and radiate warmth and love, or he or she may have some questions for you. The encounter can happen immediately after the person has passed away, or it could be years later. Furthermore, the ghost may manifest as someone you don't know, a figure from an earlier age.

It's important to realize that, psychologically-speaking, the dead do not emerge for the same "reasons." Robert Moss, author of the *Dreamer's Book of the Dead*, suggests that the spirits may have messages for dreamers, or the spirits may themselves be looking for information. Sometimes they may have messages for you to pass on to others. And of course, making contact with the dead can be cathartic if you have something to tell them that you never had the chance to say. There is a real opportunity for closure and forgiveness.

The following visitation story was first published in a Western Japanese newspaper and recently republished in *Dreaming*, the journal of the Association for the Study of Dreams:

> *"One night in July 1961, Mr. Ishida, a chief mechanic, had a dream of a sailor while he was sleeping...in the nap room at Tsuiki Airforce Base, Fukuoka Prefecture, which was a commando-type air force base during World War II. The sailor wore a uniform and said he had been killed by being caught in a spinning airplane propeller. While he was dreaming, Mr. Ishida felt a heavy weight in his breast and couldn't move an inch, though he struggled to. Mr. Ishida examined the history of this air force base and learned that there had been such an accident in the past."*[64]

Unless you discount this narrative, and others like it, completely, there is no doubt that these uncanny experiences can be healing and restorative, if not for you personally, than perhaps in service to others, or the culture at large. For those wishing to investigate ghost hauntings and sacred sites through the lens of SP/HH, a high level of empathy is necessary to witness the vision without overlaying it with our own fear projections.

Angels

Some historical accounts of angel visions sound suspiciously like sleep paralysis/hypnagogic (SP/HH) encounters, suggests consciousness researcher J.A. Cheyne. Some of these tales are hidden in our oldest and most trusted sources. In *Genesis* 32:24-32, for example, Jacob "wrestles a man until daybreak." Finally, Jacob shows he is not afraid by asking to be blessed. The figure blesses him and Jacob later interprets the experience as a meeting with an angel of the Lord. Many people have described SP as "wrestling with ghosts," and the fact that Jacob had this meeting until daybreak is a tempting signal that he was asleep when the encounter occurred.[65]

Cheyne also notes that the Muslim prophet Muhammad had some visitations that resemble sleep paralysis visions. Religion scholar Karen Armstrong describes this famous account:

"Muhammad was torn from sleep and felt himself enveloped by a devastatingly divine presence … he said that an angel had appeared to him and given him a curt command: 'Recite!'" When Muhammad refused, "the angel simply enveloped him in an overpowering embrace so that he felt as if all the breath was being squeezed from his body."

Finally, after three terrifying embraces, Muhammad relents and recites a new poem. This is the beginning of the *Qur'an*—also known as the *Koran*—which means "the Recitation." [66]

Eighteenth Century scientist and Christian mystic Emmanuel Swedenborg also wrote about angels with whom he had lengthy philosophical conversations. These visitations came at night, in dreams and visions. While the connection of SP to Swedenborg is probable, as he writes of wrestling demons in his personal dream journal,[67] he was undoubtedly a master of hypnagogia, as he wrote about how to induce vision states that "come in a state midway between sleep and wakefulness."[68]

As David Hufford reminds us, many people believe in spirits even after they learn about the physical correlates to these visions.[69] This disconnect may have historical roots. After all, science as an enterprise has stayed out of the question of meaning and subjectivity ever since the Enlightenment, when the Church threatened death to scientists who committed heresy by opining on their turf. This is, no doubt, why even Rene Descartes kept his dream journal a lifelong secret. Rationally speaking, SP/HH is where mystics have visions, the religious encounter God, and where seekers of all kinds can communicate with uncanny sources of wisdom.

Dream researcher Robert Van De Castle uses the phrase "Internalized Self Helper" for these archetypal characters that clearly have something to teach us.[70] Whether you believe divinity comes from within or from beyond, these otherworldly dream figures want to help, and SP/HH seems to be a way to communicate with them. Trust and listen carefully.

The Guided Journey

When the Stranger comes and you are not afraid, sometimes there is another opportunity: to go with the apparition on a guided dream journey. You may suddenly find yourself flying over a forest with this guardian figure or transported to a great castle where you meet a king or queen. Or you may descend into a cave beneath the earth of your present sleeping location and meet indigenous-looking peoples who are just as curious about you as you are about them. These encounters are unforgettable and can be life changing.

Here is an example of a guided journey I had several years ago. I was sleeping in the room of my fiancée's grandmother, a woman whom I'd never met nor knew much about.

> *I wake up in the bedroom and feel a presence in the room. Then I feel the presence sit down on the bed next to me. I am frightened and then I remember that my fiancée's grandmother died in this room. I relax, no longer threatened, but still a little nervous. I then see an older woman standing in front of me. She is clasping a ream of papers in front of her chest. She communicates to me that she's been doing research and has been writing stories. She doesn't speak this; it's just an understanding. She seems excited. I say to her, "Show me," and I instantly melt through the bed and am now flying*

*through a vast misty space. I then see the earth is far below
me, and I move through more layers of clouds. I'm flying but
not in control—it's like I'm being brought here. The mists
clear and I see I am flying over a glowing red ocean of lava.
Then more mists, and I fall through the sky for a long time.
I stay open to the experience: I cannot see but I trust as best
I can. Below me now is an ocean with blue rolling waves. I
land in the ocean and tread water. The sea is active with big
waves, and a storm is approaching.... I wake up.*

I told the dream over breakfast the next day to my fiancée's
parents. Her mother got very quiet when I mentioned the ream
of papers. After I finished, she told me that her mother was, in
fact, a writer in her youth but had to give up her dream of being
a writer to raise a family. She had often spoken of all the stories in
her head that she had never written down. Maybe, this was just a
coincidence. Then again, unusual coincidences, or synchronicities,
like this seem to happen a lot around SP visitations.

Recommendations for Guided Journeys

In my own guided journey, when I said, "Show me," the
encounter quickly became a lucid dream journey. It was effortless
on my part because that's where the dream-vision wanted to go.
That is the key to a successful journey: not forcing it but going
with the flow.

I recommend a guided journey only if you truly trust the
visitation figure. Trust first, but be discerning. Of course, this is a
dream, and since you have the power to keep your fear at bay, you
also always have the power to wake up when you want. All of the
dream-waking techniques from Chapter 1 are at your disposal.

Stay emotionally grounded. In the dream above, I needed to
check in with myself on several occasions and find my trust. This
inner knowledge of confidence will keep you grounded no matter
how high you fly above the earth and all the heavens. The Sleep
Paralysis Worksheet (the Appendix) will help with memorizing
your affirmation, building a plan, and remembering your core

values for moments like this.

Once you awaken, write down the account as soon as possible. In particular, try to recall the exact words that the guide said to you. Let the dream rest for a few days, and then, take a look at the account again. What was discovered? Where did the guide take you? What did you take away that you did not have before?

Alien Abduction: Journey of the Unwilling

The alien abduction narrative may be today's most misunderstood version of the guided journey. Many alien abduction accounts have the earmarks of SP, with the victims awakening in the bedroom, sensing a presence, noticing they cannot move, and finally, confronting a scary alien being. Sometimes, these accounts go on to describe how the alien takes the victim on a journey to the stars. This account almost sounds like a modern version of an angel visitation and also of centuries-old fairyland encounters. But far from pleasant, these accounts sometimes end up with the victims being tortured and sexually molested. The abduction account concludes when victims wake up in the bedroom, as if they never had left, but scared out of their wits. If these victims have never had a lucid dream before or experienced iSP, they may think the journey physically occurred.

Current research into alien abduction suggests that there is a connection between iSP, alien abduction accounts, and a past history of childhood sexual abuse.[71] Both those who report being abducted by aliens and those who have memories of abuse also report more SP. And all three groups score more highly in certain psychological traits, such as being creative, fantasy-prone, and open to paranormal experiences.

If you have a history of sexual abuse, these memories and fears may easily surface during a SP encounter. I recommend working on your courage and keeping strong boundaries when you find yourself face to face with the Stranger-as-Alien. Talking to a counselor or a psychiatrist (who knows how to work with dreams) about these troubling experiences is also a good idea.

Other SP researchers have suggested that alien abduction stories could represent traumatic memories of surgery. These accounts have many elements of the modern medical environment, in which we are held down and paralyzed in a well-lit and sterilized room, prodded against our will, and leaned over by goggled and masked entities.[72]

Folklorist and illustrator Brian Froud takes an ecopsychological approach, suggesting in his book *Good Fairies, Bad Fairies* that the eyes of the prototypical alien figure —large, dark, and fathomless— "reflect our dysfunctional relationship with the earth: our wanton misuse of nature's gifts, our exploitation of natural resources without regard for consequences, our short-sighted practice of taking from nature and not giving back."[73]

In other words, perhaps we are the aliens. In all three of these renderings, as sexual abuse, as surgical memories, and as a symptom of ecological devastation, the theme is one of something lost, something damaged, and something that was once alive and now destroyed. This is the dark side of the guided journey, but it is not merely a replay of something unfixable, either inside us or in our culture. As dreamworker Jeremy Taylor says, all dreams come in the service of health and wholeness and not simply to point out all the things about yourself and the world that are broken and cannot be addressed.[74] Like all nightmares, including ones related to Post-traumatic stress disorder,[75] the visions of iSP are signals to "pay attention—this is important."

The Near-Death Experience Connection

Journeys during iSP also sometimes resemble accounts of Near Death Experience.[76] Coined by Raymond Moody, the NDE is an experience that happens at the threshold between life and death or when someone is frightened that death is about to come.[77] The contents of the visions are phenomenologically similar: white light experiences, contact with entities, angels, ancestors, the recently dead and religious figures, and the life review, like the one that Ebenezer Scrooge endures. It is possible that the extreme fear and death anxiety that accompanies iSP may trigger this natural vision state. Recent neurological studies in NDE suggest that these experiences are accompanied by REM intrusion into waking consciousness,[78] just like iSP hallucinations, although the evidence is preliminary at best.

In my mind, NDEs do not answer the question of whether or not there is an afterlife, but rather suggest that, under extreme duress, we generate meaningful visions that provide guidance, hope, and sometimes, validity for the terror about our present condition. However, the uncanny content of these visions - such as telepathy or remote viewing - is an aspect of the NDE phenomenon that cannot be explained in total by today's science, unless we disregard thousands of reputable accounts by individuals around the world.

A less reported version of the classic NDE is known as the frightening NDE. These visions, like positive NDEs, happen when the patient is near death, but the content of the vision is not reassuring at all, including Hell-like imagery, pain, the sounds of screaming and torture, and the presence of lifeless or threatening apparitions.[79] Due to stigma, these types of experiences are probably under-reported, just like frightening SP hallucinations. Another similarity between these two states is that they are often thought to be physically "real," as the dreamer may not know that it's possible to have a vision and still be in his "right mind." Both NDE and SP guided journeys may be influenced by your attitude and interpretation of the event as it unfolds, which is why building courage and developing compassion is crucial in the inner worlds and in waking life.

Part III:
Thriving with Sleep Paralysis

CHAPTER SIX

Extraordinary Dreams And Visions

Isolated sleep paralysis is a blessing in disguise. Once you have mastered the basics in controlling breath and fear, you have a unique opportunity that most people in the world never get a chance to experience: dreaming consciously. This state of consciousness is lucid dreaming, of course, which was scientifically validated in the laboratory by dream researcher Stephen LaBerge.

What else can we call SP but a gateway to lucid dreaming? We know our bodies are asleep and simultaneously we are participating in the dreaming world. Psychologist Jorge Conesa-Sevilla uses the term "bound lucidity."[80] Once SP is understood, and you have made contact with your core beliefs so you feel safe, you can easily learn how to focus on dreams you *want* to have and watch them materialize around you.

What would you dream if given the chance to do anything? Anything at all - no physical limits, no financial limits, nothing in between you and your greatest fantasy? The only thing that can limit the possibilities in conscious dreaming is a poverty of intention by not knowing what you want to do.

So let's look at some of the amazing experiences that can be had once you realize you are in SP.

Out-of-Body Experiences

The experience of being out-of-body has been recounted for thousands of years. Whether you believe that the soul is actually separating from the body or that it is a simulation based on sensations from the brain, out-of-body experiences (OBEs) are highly linked to sleeping and dreaming states.[81] Many people start their journeys while lying in bed, and when the experience is over, they wake up safe and sound.

Sleep paralysis is a reliable launching pad to an OBE. The powerful feelings of being crushed, twisted, or pulled along are a good indicator that you can separate your mind (the "I" or the seat of your personal perspective) from these bodily sensations. According to SP expert David Hufford, OBEs are more likely to emerge after SP experiences that last at least 2 minutes.[82]

Here's an example of an SP-to-OBE I had recently. I was sleep deprived (jetlagged actually) and knew that if I took a nap lying on my back I could probably have a SP. It worked like a charm. Here's the account:

> *I hear a rushing sound in my ears; it comes and goes like ocean waves. I focus on my ears so the rushing increases; it comes back in longer and longer durations. Finally, the rushing sensation is constant and I hear a distinct tone as well, like a bell. I try to move but cannot. "I am in sleep paralysis," I think. I then try to move out of my body. I try to go up but it seems blocked, so I kick myself out to the left and down. It's an odd sensation; my "me" leaves a part behind. As soon as I'm "out," everything changes. It is quiet, cool, and dark. I feel like I'm drifting down a stream. I have a small fear arise, and then, I relax into the sensation... it's very calming. Some lights like stars are overhead. My breathing is slow and deep. After a while, I decide to go back. I wriggle my little toe (which I cannot see because I am still floating down a dark river!) but the focus brings me back. After a few seconds, I can move and I open my eyes.*

Note how I calmed my fears, noticed my breath, and finally used the tried-and-true toe wiggle method to wake myself up. With a little practice, these techniques become second nature.

Techniques for OBEs

Focus on the Belly

This tactic was devised by Jorge Conesa-Sevilla. When you are in SP, focus on your belly. Specifically focus right underneath the navel. Now imagine your body is "rolling up" into that spot. If the feeling of pressure increases just on that spot, but nowhere else, then you are doing it right. When the pressure increases, again use your attention to just "roll" out of your body. You may feel a "pop" as the mind dissociates from body feelings. From here, you can go on to have an out-of-body experience or simply wake up from the dream.

The Sit-Up Trick

This method works for a friend of mine who is an advanced dream adventurer. When he feels he is in SP, he focuses his intention by concentrating on the spot between his eyes, and then, he tries to do a sit-up. Of course, he's in SP, so he can't actually sit up. But if the intention is strong enough, rather than waking up, you can "pop" right out of your physical body and float around.

A Note Concerning Fear During OBEs

OBEs are weird. Even veteran explorers of the inner worlds say that OBEs feel different than the usual dream. They feel more real than real. Sometimes, you may get scared, especially if you start floating off into the sky and have the thought, "What if I never come back?" Like many aspects of conscious dreaming, your beliefs can greatly affect your experience. Sometimes our beliefs can be limiting ("That's impossible!"), but they can also be grounding ("I trust that I cannot be hurt because I am dreaming").

Unexamined beliefs are the wild cards: These act as subconscious expectations that can really hijack a conscious dream.[83] Take a moment and reflect on what you believe about out-of-body experiences. Do you believe in a soul? Do you believe in life after death? What about reincarnation? Are you in fear of a final judgment? Is the OBE a trick of the brain, a "virtual reality" owing more to synapses than to souls? These are the kinds of thoughts that can greatly influence your OBE, negatively or positively. Sometimes, an unexamined belief can actually cause a serious crisis of faith in the middle of these experiences. So, the more you have considered these deep questions, the more comfortable you will be in this profound altered state.

When all else fails, wake up!

Just like a conscious dream or SP proper, you can will yourself to wake up whenever you want during an OBE. Control your breath; control your fear. Also, focusing on one point for a few moments is a good way to disrupt an OBE and lead you closer to snapping back to the "real world," whatever that means anymore.

Lucid Dreaming

Lucid dreams occur when you realize that you are dreaming while still asleep. SP is really a special kind of lucid dream in which you are awake and aware during the muscle atonia of sleep onset, rather than in the middle of a dream.

Just as you can launch into an OBE during SP, you can also move further into the dreamworld and keep your awareness. These amazing experiences have been scientifically demonstrated in the sleep laboratory, despite years of medical doubt.[84] Stanford researcher Stephen LaBerge has also shown that lucid dreaming is a learnable skill and has spent much of his career devising effective methods to become lucid. Many people say lucid dreaming is the most exciting and profound times of their lives. The good news is that those who have iSP make excellent lucid dreamers.

What can you do during a lucid dream? Well, that is really up to you. The two most popular activities for new lucid dreamers are 1) to fly around and 2) to have a sexual adventure. It's been demonstrated in the sleep lab that lucid dream orgasms are physiologically real, too.

Lucid dreaming is more than a virtual playground, however. You can also go looking for someone who has passed on or rehearse an activity that you want to learn in waking life. Or you can meditate and possibly experience what mystics and visionaries have been writing poetry about for eons. The ability to have ecstatic visions and even a taste of enlightenment is why lucid dreaming is considered an avenue into "peak experiences."

A word to the wise about seeking the divine in lucid dreams: dream researcher Fariba Bogzaran has shown that actively seeking for God is more likely to end merely with a scenario that mimics what the dreamer anticipates—showcasing the power of expectation. However, if you surrender control and ask to experience the Divine, you are more likely to be shown something unexpected... and possibly life-changing.[85]

The Dark Side of Lucid Dreaming

When exploring SP to lucid dreaming, be prepared for unpleasant experiences. This is the dark side of lucid dreaming that is not often talked about.[86] When you know you are dreaming, but decide to open up to the unknown, the door with the most pressure behind it opens first. So if there is an issue in your life that you have succeeded so far in repressing, welcome to the dream world, where there is no hiding. Dreaming is an intense state of mind, fueled by titanic drives, strong emotions, vivid imagery, and unparalleled access to long-term memories. When you add self-awareness to the mix, the result can be what anthropologist Michael Winkelman calls "shamanic consciousness."[87] In other words, some lucid dream themes resemble closely the historic and cross-cultural accounts of the vision states of the world's first medicine men and healers. The most consistent themes here include ritual sacrifice, death, mutilation, and rebirth. These dreams can be seen as personal initiations. They seem to come at the cross-roads in our lives, and in this ancient intersection, we are open to influences that may extend far beyond our personal psychology. These experiences are powerful and can be healing in themselves.[88]

The Jewel Dream

This SP narrative was collected from a dreamer named Tjalle who lies in the Middle East. Her courage is astounding as she faces her own initiation.

> *I was reading for a while, then I noticed that the wall (about 6 feet from the end of my bed) started to sort of wobble. My body was paralyzed, unable to move. My breathing was kind of non-existent, though I desperately needed more air. Suddenly, it opened up into a black void. Like a 9 ft black hole, vaguely the shape of a figure. "O my god," I thought, "I am dreaming. This can't be true." The black-hole sort of oozed into the room. I was beyond terror. I still don't understand how my heart didn't collapse. The blackness started molding itself into a recognizable shape. It became a 9 ft tall Japanese devil or devilish looking Samurai. Viciously grinning he said, "You are not dreaming. You thought you could 'integrate me.'" He then, in one sweeping movement, stretched out his enormous black hand, grabbed me, stuffed me into his blood-red mouth, and swallowed me. Then I fell into unconsciousness for a moment, now a vortex pulled me down into an abyss of no dimensions. All of a sudden, I was spat back out into his hand. Somehow, I had crystallized into a red ruby. I WAS a ruby; I felt like a ruby. So there I was, in the big hand of a giant, looking at him, and he looking at me. In that moment—seeing each other—something happened. We looked at each other, became truly aware of each other, and then, there was love. I know what the mystics talk about/can't talk about. There is believing, and then, there is knowing.*

Going Lucid from Sleep Paralysis

Similar to an OBE, it is easy to emerge in a full lucid dream from SP. After you have centered yourself, close your eyes. Relax into the strange floating sensations and go with the flow. Now draw up your intention and make a declaration. "I want to fly over the ocean!" Imagine yourself there. If you are still in the dream state, the dream will emerge from the darkness of your closed eyes. The dream will actually crystallize around you until it seems as real as waking life. Remind yourself, "I'm dreaming," and notice how clear your mind feels, how real the sensations feel, and how bright the colors are.

Sometimes, the dream imagery is not strong enough to match our intention. A good way to test the "reality" of the imagery is to wave your hand in front of your face. Your dream hand, I mean, because your physical hand is actually paralyzed. At first, you may only see a light shape moving through the darkness. When you can clearly see your hand, then you know you are ready to move into lucid dreaming.[89]

Another trick that works for many others and myself is to imagine a vortex or a doorway in my minds eye. Once I see the vortex, I "will" myself to enter it. After going through a tunnel made of colorful lights, I emerge into a lucid dream. What is useful about this method is that you can use it when you have a strong intention for a particular dream or if you just want to see where you will end up.[90]

Have a Plan

Whatever you do, it's best to have a plan for your intentions in the dream before you go to bed. Otherwise, the lucid dream may not last very long. I encourage you to determine what it is that you would like to experience with all your mind and your heart. Rather than a "Gee, this would be neat," go for "I deeply yearn to know what it feels like to…" If the intention is strong enough, you will remember it when you enter a dream from SP. Keep the intention open-ended for best results. For instance, for beginners, flying to the moon may end in failure if that is a difficult concept to visualize once you get going, but deciding to fly (in general, with no set destination) will be more successful because it is more open to the dream's feedback. The lucid dream is, after all, co-created. It's a creative collaboration, not a holodeck.

The Stranger in Lucid Dreams

If the Stranger has already manifested during the SP and you try to use a lucid dream to escape, the apparition may follow you into the dream. This is because fear is deeper than whatever dream scene we happen to be in. Don't run from the apparition, but ground yourself and practice your compassion and your trust. You are safe, and the dream cannot show you anything you are not prepared to accept, even though sometimes that means facing unpleasant truths.

If you feel unsafe in the dream still, walk to someplace that you can stand your ground more confidently. For example, I sometimes climb a hill in a dream when I am preparing to meet something unknown. In some cases, the Stranger will transform again and have something to show or tell. This figure can later become an ally for future dreams, or someone you can call on for when you have a question for the dreamworld.

Sexual Hallucinations: The Succubus Revisited

The historic fears of succubi and incubi must be reconsidered in light of contemporary psychology. As the medical community disregarded the narratives of SP until David Hufford's ground-breaking work in the 1970s, we would be making the same mistake if we chalk up the old tales of sexual demons to "merely legend."

Modern dreamers still have sexual experiences in sleep paralysis, and ghost rape remains a phenomenon that is whispered about in anonymous and private settings. I have already discussed how alien encounters are one popular interpretation of the sensations of being forcibly touched by an entity (seen and unseen) while paralyzed in bed. Other cultural interpretations today include demons of the devil (evangelical Christianity) and a visit by the spirit form of a dark magician (indigenous shamanism).[91] Jungian psychologists may interpret spectral rape as a vampire complex, representing an imbalanced relationship with the parent of the opposite sex or perhaps hinting at memories of incest.[92] As suggested in Chapter 5, dreamers with a history of sexual abuse may be more likely to experience flashbacks during SP/HH. Similarly, survivors of trauma also may incorporate flashbacks into HH.[93] However it is viewed, I think it is important to not interpret away the actual encounter. These things happen and they are a natural, although disturbing, part of human experience.

The physiology of the dream state may be one reason why sexual content is so often reported. In the REM state, our muscles are in paralysis, but the body is in a state of excitement. Men typically get erections, and women's genitalia become engorged. Orgasms have been documented countless times in dream labs, and in lucid dreams, it is possible to experience orgasm, too. Dreaming sleep is simply a sexy place to be. Even when we are scared, and sometimes *because* we are scared, sexual excitement does not diminish. Sexuality and terror are deeply intertwined, neurologically speaking. So it's not that outlandish to believe the medieval court documents in which men tell of being forced to have sex with mysterious she-demons and witches, even though this testimony was used in service of misogyny and the destruction of indigenous religious practices.

However, some sexual SP/HH encounters are not necessarily unpleasant. For dreamers who do not have a traumatized past, sexual play during hypnagogic hallucinations can be healthy and exciting. This was brought to my attention when one reader from my website admitted that he cherishes the ephemeral spirits who approach him at night. He reports excitement, pleasure, and mental orgasms during his SP-induced hallucinations. He does not seek these escapades but does not seem to mind too much, even though he admits it somewhat strange that the spirit sometimes is not altogether human. In *Dark Intrusions*, Louis Proud also has collected reports of spectral sex that are erotic, albeit deeply weird. As with lucid dreaming, sensuality can be safely explored in this private mental arena.[94] Still, Proud writes, "I do have my suspicions as to whether or not 'spirit sex' is entirely wholesome."[95]

Like Proud, I can't recommend treating these experiences like a fantasy world. There are always psychological repercussions to any act, thought, or way of being. Also, as with lucid dreaming and waking life, these encounters can be more pleasurable if they are not goal-oriented, but rather based on intimacy and consensual action. If the encounter gets too weird, or compromises your safe boundaries, you can always wake up using the methods described in Chapter 1.

As with all vision-states, one can become addicted to the inner adventure at the expense of healthy waking life. Psychologists call the unhealthy drive for ecstatic states *spiritual bypass*, and this concept may be at the root of the historically-noted danger of falling in love with the spirits and nymphs of the inner world. After all, what ordinary and flawed human partner can compete with an alluring fantasy lover who comes only at night?

Sexual demons can reveal patterns in our romantic life, especially concerning how we give of ourselves. For men, repeated encounters with sexual vampires who seem to suck up inner resources or willpower may be reflective of an unhealthy sexual pattern in waking life. This encounter illustrates a leak of life force that may be unsustainable. For women, not being able to stop the sexual advances of a night demon may be indicative of difficulties in drawing firm boundaries or deciding who is allowed to enter your sphere. Of course, these visions of energy imbalance (of chi-sucking and demon rape) can work for either gender, depending on character, personal history, sexual orientation, and gender identity.

In spite of these dangers, rest assured that in the 21st century no one will condemn you in a court of law for having intercourse with a night elf or a water pixie.

Hypnagogia and the Creative Mind

Visionary SP occurs during sleep onset, also known as hypnagogia. A sister state, hypnopompia, happens during arousal from sleep. For most people, these stages of consciousness are a 20-second blip of sounds and imagery and usually are not remembered. For SP explorers, however, hypnagogia and hypnopompia can last upwards of 20 minutes. The features of these altered states include visual and auditory hallucinations, feelings of floating and falling, and occasionally other senses like smells and touch. You may see a kaleidoscope of imagery, hear music, or experience a combination of senses, such as "feeling colors" or "hearing images."

Edgar Allan Poe wrote that hypnagogic images "arise in the soul...at those mere points in time when the confines of the waking world blend with those of the world of dreams."[96] Hypnagogia, like lucid dreams, are in between worlds so that the conscious mind can witness and explore the inner worlds with clarity.

This state of consciousness is a powerful way to access the creative mind. Many of the famous so-called "problem-solving" dreams, such as the discovery of the shape of the benzene molecule, actually took place in sleep onset.[97] Artists have also tapped this rich source of imagery. For example, surrealist painter Salvador Dali brought back many of his bizarre dream-like images from hypnagogia by falling asleep in his armchair while holding a key. When he went through sleep onset, his hand dropped, causing the key to clatter to the floor and awaken him—but not before he had experienced some dream imagery to inspire his next painting.[98] The inventor Thomas Edison had a similar system: in his case, he held steel balls in his hand and would awaken as they dropped onto a pan.[99]

I personally know several dream artists who literally find their next painting in their lucid dreams. One friend tells me he walks into an art gallery in his dream and looks at the paintings on the wall. He memorizes every detail and then wakes up and makes a quick sketch of what he has seen.

Classical music geniuses Mozart and Beethoven also claimed

73

to hear music in their dreams. I have experienced dozens of original musical compositions in the hypnagogic state; the effect is incredible because the sound is three-dimensional. I could choose to just listen or focus on a specific instrument and guide a solo. In this way, I have been bathed in lucid compositions of jazz, rock'n roll, and even some excellent down-tempo dark wave techno.

If you are working on a difficult problem, such as a complex algorithm or an organizational puzzle, try focusing on it during SP hallucinations. The perfect balance is to use the conscious mind to focus on the problem in the first place but then step back and allow the creative mind to play. When you wake up, write down what you have experienced, and then, see if any insights can be gleaned from it.

This is precisely how Elias Howe invented the modern sewing machine. He fell asleep at his work desk and had a dream that he was going to be boiled alive by head-hunters. He woke up as they jabbed their spears in his face. Upon awakening, he remembered that the natives' spears had a peculiar hole near the top of the shaft. This turned out to be the creative answer to Howe's dilemma about how to construct the sewing needle for his new machine.[100]

Sleep paralysis is a reliable portal to these creative states. The dreaming mind will crunch any problem you give it, provided you can enter hypnagogia and maintain your awareness. Again, it's important to have a plan before you nap. Use the included worksheet to draft some of your strongest intentions, and with patience, these seeds can be planted in the rich soil of the conscious dream.

CHAPTER SEVEN
Increasing The Odds Of Sleep Paralysis

Allow me one more disclaimer before launching into this material. While isolated SP is not a health risk in itself, it can stir up emotional and psychological issues with regard to beliefs, safe boundaries and the meaning of the life. SP may instigate other destabilizing spiritual experiences. As a gateway to extraordinary dreams, SP also can retrigger strong emotional memories from childhood.

So, if you are ready to dive into these deep waters, I recommend that you evaluate your life situation before leaving the ground. Do you really have the time to explore these states of consciousness? Do you have a network of friends that you can discuss your experiences with? Do you have a stable home life with access to a safe place to sleep? Do you have an older or more experienced mentor to reach out to in case of spiritual emergency—such as a minister, psychotherapist, a wise aunt or uncle, or spiritual coach? These are important considerations before embarking on a quest into the underworld of the visionary mind.[101]

I'm not just covering myself here. I have personally had destabilizing lucid dream experiences that occurred simultaneously with profound digestive troubles. It was a painful ordeal, and only after fasting with water and lemon juice for 4 days did things return to normal. Perhaps, metaphorically, I could not digest what was happening. Kenneth Kezler, in his lucid dreaming classic *The Sun and the Shadow*, reports a similar story of bodily destabilization due to not being prepared for his lucid journeys.

Now when I prepare for a SP or lucid dream incubation or if I feel it is coming on spontaneously, I limit alcohol, sugar, meat, and processed grains in my diet. I tell my closest friends (and most recently, my wife) what I am attempting, so I will be looked after. I limit exposure to TV, violent imagery in the media and spend more time in nature. These precautions serve to stabilize myself so I can encounter the visionary dreams with a courageous heart and an open mind.

The tactics below are for the most intrepid explorers of consciousness. They can be useful for fieldwork in paranormal investigations too. Knowing the causes of SP can greatly increase the chance of an uncanny encounter when sleeping for a night in an old house that is reputed to be haunted or when camping near historic or sacred grounds.

Tactics for Triggering Sleep Paralysis

Many of the ways to bring on SP is to use your knowledge of the causes of SP and move towards them rather than away from them. The most reliable method is to use the body's own REM rebound effect after REM deprivation.

- Sleep on your back.
- Take a nap after being sleep deprived or jet-lagged.
- Keep an erratic sleep pattern.
- Maximize REM rebound by waking up 2 hours before normal and then nap.

For example, if I stay up late to finish a project and I am sleep deprived the next day, I purposefully take an afternoon nap sleeping on my back. This mix of situation, posture, and desire is almost guaranteed to bring on an episode of SP.

Travel is also highly effective for bringing SP on. The jet lag, the culture shock, and the scattering of daily habits makes for an open heart. Going to sleep in unusual places also brings on extraordinary dreams. So always keep the journal close at hand when traveling.

Dream Supplements for Encouraging SP

Caffeine

Thomas Yuschak, an expert lucid dreamer, suggests that low doses of caffeine before bed will inhibit deep sleep but still permit sleep onset and light sleep. This is an easy way to heighten the chance of experiencing SP while falling asleep. He recommends 50 mg of caffeine an hour before bed. The technique is more effective if paired with a REM booster, such as galantamine.[102]

Galantamine

This is a plant-derived supplement that works by preventing the breakdown of acetylcholine. This important neurotransmitter lengthens the REM (dreaming) phase of sleep and, at heightened levels, increases dream recall, dream vividness, and lucid dreaming. One of the main side effects of galantamine is that it also promotes SP.[103] I have tested galantamine extensively and have found it to dramatically boost the chances of having SP as a prelude to a lucid dream.

Choline

Choline is brain fuel, heightening the effect of galantamine by providing more acetylcholine in the brain. An amino acid found in many common foods, such as eggs, bananas, and potatoes, it's also cheaply found over-the-counter as soy lecithin.

Calea Zachatechichi

Known as "the dream herb," this potent botanical has been used for centuries in Mexico as a dream enhancer. Specifically, calea heightens the vividness of hypnagogic imagery. It also decreases REM sleep, which of course will instigate a REM rebound later. So calea is helpful coming and going.

Mental Practices for Increasing SP, OBEs, Hypnagogic Reverie, and Lucid Dreams

The following are mental practices and tactics useful in inducing creative HH and lucid dreaming from SP. They are all variations on a single theme, namely: focus. We are all wired a little differently, so taken together these methods display a range of tactics at your disposal, depending on your interests, as well as your own special abilities.

Wake-Initiated Sleep Paralysis (WISP)
This method is my derivation of the wake-initiated-lucid-dream (WILD) method, popularized by Stephen LaBerge and Howard Rheingold in their classic book *Exploring the World of Lucid Dreaming.* I have found that the most reliable way to induce iSP is directly from the waking state.

WISP by Auditory Cues
Here's an auditory way into WISP that works for me. If you have good balance and are prone to auditory hallucinations during hypnagogia, this method is recommended. After closing your eyes, focus on a spot in the middle of your visual field. Notice the lights and colors as they come and go, but don't follow them. Also pay attention to vibrations or quick "rushing" sounds in your ears. The "rush" may be accompanied by an electric shiver down your body or other sensations from your head down the groin. With a little practice, you can increase the vibrations by willing it to come back until the rushing vibration is a constant. You are now in paralysis––try to move to confirm it. This is how I enter SP directly from the waking state.

WISP by Vortex
This is the method I have used as early as six years old to fall asleep, which just goes to show that children are natural visionaries. Lying on your back, close your eyes, and focus your

attention in between and slightly above the eyes. When the lights and imagery begin to swim around, keep the focus. After a while, the spectral lights will gather around your point of concentration, like a kaleidoscope. Keep the focus, but *will* yourself to enter this imagery. With practice, if you are now in sleep onset, the imagery will expand and envelope the visual field. This imagery forms a vortex and often is associated with those vestibular hallucinations of falling or flying. Go through the tunnel and enter the dream.

Nap and Mantra-assisted SP

Ben Phillips, one of my DreamStudies.org readers and a sleep paralysis expert in his own right, has this method to share. Essentially, he recommends taking a nap to disrupt your normal sleep patterns, and then using a spoken word, or mantra, to assist in falling asleep with awareness.

Here is Phillip's full method, in his own words:

1. Wake up earlier than normal
2. Stay awake for the whole day; go to work, school or if you're unemployed, do something active.
3. Between 7 and 10 p.m., have a nap. This nap must be no longer than 2 hours. An hour and a half should suffice. It is important that once you wake up from the nap, you don't close your eyes or snooze, if you do you will dream and the chance of strong SP later will be diminished. Set an alarm or ask someone to wake you up.
4. Stay awake for at least an hour, no more than four.
5. Go to bed. When you lay down... any position will do, close your eyes and get comfortable. There are no particular meditative exercises to follow as long as you simply relax your body and lie as still as you can.
6. When you are relaxed and your mind is settled, simply think of a name or a word... it can be any word.
7. Repeat the word over and over again in your head. Imagine the word being spoken to you. Think of nothing else. Listen for

the word in the quietness of your head.

8. Do not pay any attention to any hypnagogic light blooms, only the sound of yourself imagining the word.

9. After a short period of this concentrated listening, the word should start to take on a life of its own and will probably be accompanied by other auditory sensations, such as intermittent bursts of rumbling, wooshing, and a spatial hiss. There will be a distinct shift in awareness and perception. You are at this point on the threshold of Sleep Paralysis.

Middle-of-the-Night Meditation

This next method is taught by psychotherapist and lucid dreaming pioneer Scott Sparrow.[104] It is based on the centuries old traditions of Tibetan Dream Yoga. Set your alarm to wake up in the middle of the night. Sit up in bed and do 10-15 minutes of concentrative meditation or breathwork. Prayer is also effective, especially long prayers that you have memorized. Then, as you settle back to sleep, recall your intention to stay aware as you fall asleep (whether to enter an OBE, have great hypnagogic imagery, or enter a lucid dream—your choice).

Middle-of-the-Night Reading

A variation of Sparrow's method is to set your alarm to wake you up in the middle of the night. You need to time your awakening for 3 or 4.5 hours after you fall asleep. Wake up, turn on a small bed light, and open up a book on lucid dreaming or some other subject matter you find fascinating. Read for 10-15 minutes, and then go back to sleep. A variation that has worked for me is to journal about my intentions for 10-15 minutes. Then, use the WISP method to remain aware as you fall asleep. This method works because reading activates the part of the brain that also regulates self-awareness and critical thinking: the forebrain and parietal lobes.

Sleep Paralysis Signaling

Sleep Paralysis Signaling (SPS) was devised by Jorge Conesa Sevilla, author of *Wrestling with Ghosts*.[105] Sevilla's method is especially effective for launching directly into a lucid dream from iSP, although you can set an intention for a OBE as well.

Phase one: When you realize you are in muscle atonia, start breathing "purposely and calmly." At the same time, focus on a part of your body, such as the belly or chest area.

Phase two: Imagine your body spinning around the navel or whatever central body part that is your object of focus. This will bring on the "vortex effect" that I mentioned in the WISP method.

Phase three: Go into the tunnel, still practicing your breath to keep fears calm, and emerge through the end of the tunnel into a dream. Take special care to remind yourself "I am dreaming" when you enter the new dream space. From here, you can interact as you choose.

Starting a Mindful Practice

In general, researchers have also found that having a mental/spiritual practice reduces stress and alleviates anxiety.[106] In fact, many health practitioners have found that the best way to stay healthy is to treat not just our bodies, but to also nourish our hearts and souls.

If you have never done mental/spiritual practices before, the most effective approach is to find an activity that links back to your culture-of-origin. The second quickest approach is to find a spiritual practice that you can do without having to accept a new religion along with it. For example, you can learn how to meditate, or take a daily silent walk in the woods. Yoga is more popular than ever as an exercise routine, and it's great for toning the body and the mind at the same time.

One of my preferred practices is nature awareness.[107] This can be done in a city park on lunch break or during a long immersion program. The habit is more important than the quality of "pristine wilderness" you have access to. I simply sit down comfortably, and with a soft-focus, watch and look and listen and smell, while at the same time I track my feelings and thoughts. This practice is especially good for soothing alienation. It also can be adapted to intuitive evaluations at sacred sites or historic places, making a powerful pair with sleep paralysis investigations: for stalking intuition by day and night. My nature awareness meditation is included in Appendix B.

Many spiritual practices focus on breathing techniques. These are especially helpful for SP because these nightmares often come with difficulties in breathing.

If you don't know how to meditate, here's some information and a beginner practice that is easy to learn. A simple meditation practice can be done before bed or whenever you are feeling stressed out. This technique can be used no matter what you believe.

My advice: Practice the breathing meditation below for 10 minutes a day to make it a habit.

A simple breathing meditation

Set a timer for 10 minutes, and while you're at it, make sure you've turned off your cellphone ringer. Sit upright comfortably. It doesn't have to be cross-legged, but you don't want to be lounging either. A little pillow underneath your seat can ease the pressure on your knees.

Breathe inward, using your nose. Focus your attention on the breath, and count the breath. Then exhale normally, focusing attention on the outward breath.

If your thoughts stray, don't worry. Just say "Not now," and resume paying attention to your breath. Breathe and count until the alarm goes off.

If you are new to meditation, those first sessions may seem like you didn't do much good. Don't worry, if you do this practice every day or even a few times a week, it will become more natural and you will experience fewer distracting thoughts. This an easy practice to blend into your lucid dreaming rituals. And most importantly, you will feel more grounded and relaxed as you explore life with more lucidity... which is the real point of all this, right? Lucid dreaming can only lead to lucid living.

Conclusion: The Private Initiation

Ultimately, this guide is meant to help bring sleep paralysis and its hallucinations into balance. With an open heart and an inquisitive mind, this natural vision state can be transformative.

As self-aware uncanny dreamers, we often must go through a private initiation before we can taste the fruits that come from the ordeal of SP. The initiation is different for everyone, but it bears the familiar calling cards of fear, self-doubt, crises of faith, and confrontations with unpleasant truths. This process will ensue regardless of culture or religious affiliation. However, once we learn to control our fears, examine our core beliefs, and have courage when facing the unknown, we become different people. We are more self-aware and more willing to take emotional risks. The dreaming arts can lead us through this growth process naturally and throughout our lives.

When viewed as an initiation into mature adulthood, SP becomes not a burden, but an opportunity to develop the mind, strengthen the heart, and feed the soul. Initiated dreamers have a lot to offer the world.

This process takes place across the entire lifespan, so be patient. Isolated SP tends to occur in most individuals a few times a year. Once the fear has been demolished, dreamers cherish these moments. When SP comes too often, take another look at the lifestyle concerns outlined in Part I and see how you can simplify or de-stress you life. On the other hand, if you want to induce the experience on purpose and feel like you have a safe home environment to do so, review Chapter 7.

Sleep paralysis is a portal to all the dreaming worlds. The question is not so much, *which world do I want to enter,*

but

which one do I want to explore first?

APPENDIX A:
Sleep Paralysis Management Worksheet

> This worksheet is a way to cement your plan of action the next time you wake up in sleep paralysis. This is not a test—there are no right or wrong answers. Writing down your intentions and reviewing them before bed, especially if you are close to sleep, will increase the likelihood the plan is remembered. The second part of the worksheet is for those suffering from a crisis in faith.

SP Affirmation

The next time you wake up in paralysis, remind yourself that SP is a natural condition of sleep and that you are not in physical danger. Writing this reminder out as an affirmation will help you remember. Using your own words, write your affirmation below.

_____

_____

_____

_____

_____

_____

_____

Course of Action

What would you like to do most if you enter sleep paralysis? Is waking up your goal, or do you wish to explore the dream state without fear? Or are you interested in having an out-of-body experience? Make a plan now about what you want to do when you next enter SP. Firmly resolve to remember it when you next find yourself in SP.

_____

_____

_____

Three Ways to Wake Up

If waking up is your goal, write down three ways from Chapter One to break SP and wake up. Choose only three. Afterwards, take a moment and close your eyes and visualize what you will do. For instance, you could repeat your Affirmation, and then, you will take three deep breaths and relax. Then, wiggle your toe and wake up. Practice this after going to bed as well if you are feeling fearful of going to sleep.

1._____

2._____

3._____

Focus on an Ally or Loved One

Choose someone who you feel safe around or someone who calms you down when you are in their presence. This could also be a religious figure for whom you have great admiration and great love. When you are feeling fearful, either before going to sleep or while in paralysis, focus on this person and your love/admiration for him or her.

Who is your ally when you need reassurance in SP?

Designate a Friend to Call

Designating a friend or relative to call in the middle of the night is a reassuring last defense. Write your suggestion here, and make sure to ask their permission.

Reviewing Your Core Beliefs

> This last exercise takes at least an hour and is designed for those who are undergoing a crisis of faith instigated by sleep paralysis. Prepare by turning off all potential distractions, and make sure you have access to a setting where you will not be disturbed. This exercise can also be performed in a group setting with discussion and sharing afterwards. If possible, go through this exercise in a natural setting, such as at a table in a park or in the backyard where you are interacting with the natural elements.

I was raised in the religious/spiritual tradition of _____

_____

In this tradition, the way to ask for help or protection is to _____

_____

_____

As an adult, I have studied or been influenced by the religious, spiritual, and scientific traditions of _____

_____

In these traditions, the way(s) to ask for help or protection is to

_____

_____

_____

15 Minute Reflection and Free Write

Now explore the relationship between your childhood and adult beliefs. What no longer holds true? And what are the shared values? More specifically, how do you find love and self-acceptance? You may want to use a separate piece of paper and free write for 10 -15 minutes, without worry of editing or perfection. Just write whatever comes to mind. It's completely normal if this exercise brings on feelings of anger or loneliness, and it may bring on new discoveries and connections too. Take a break, and then, come back and underline the statements that feel especially truthful, even if they feel raw, clichéd, or simplistic.

Now, write a few statements addressing how you find safety and security in the world that are true from both your childhood and adult perspectives. Rather than focusing on what you don't believe anymore, focus on what you *do* believe.

_____

_____

_____

_____

_____

_____

_____

This is your core belief statement that connects you to your sense of inner strength. Because this statement calms fears of the unknown, it can become an affirmation to draw upon during sleep paralysis.

APPENDIX B:

Nature Observation

Reconnecting with nature is not as hard as people make it out to be. It doesn't take pristine wilderness, a week hunting feral pigs with spears, or even an encyclopedic knowledge of all the birds in your area.

All it takes is a little time every week to go outside, close to home, and re-tune your awareness to what's happening outside. I call this nature observation, but it is really about paying attention to the wisdom of our bodily intelligence. The good news is that it doesn't take long to reconnect with our inner nature (intuition) and our outer nature (the world we live in).

In other words, the practice is about coming home to our senses. Time spent outside quickly cuts through unproductive thought and allows us easy access to our emotional intelligence and other sensory abilities that are usually repressed in our carefully pruned all-human world.

This simple technique can provide us with a more accurate understanding of ourselves and others, as well as the systems we inhabit together. The practice can be done in the backyard, during quiet moments at the office, or even, in time, during heated council circles.

Step 1. For beginners, find a quiet place outdoors where you are physically comfortable. Choose a spot close to a varied setting, such as the edge of a patch of woods, or near a stream, or bird feeder. You want to be comfortable, but alert.

Step 2. Focus inward, close your eyes if need be. Ask yourself a question like, "What is going on with me right now?" Scan your body for any fuzzy, indistinct feelings of unease. These usually are "nagging feelings" in the throat, chest, or belly. Note: this feeling is not an emotion, but is somewhat harder to "capture." But if distinct emotions come up, sit with them briefly, acknowledge them, and scan again.

Step 3. Try to find a word, phrase, or image that expresses this indistinct feeling in the body. If you lose the feeling, go back to scanning until you can feel it again. Sometimes, if the right word or association makes contact, a change in the feeling occurs. Eugene Gendlin called this a *felt shift*. It may be a shiver down your back, an insight, or an emotional release into laughter/tears. Above all, have compassion for yourself and others. A felt shift doesn't happen every time.

Step 4. After 10 minutes or so of focusing (and you will get better at it), readjust your body and shift your attention to include your surroundings, as well as your body. Keep your gaze centered, but soft, so that you are taking in peripheral vision. Notice sounds, smells, the feel of the breeze, and that spot on your knee that really itches. Go ahead and do what you need to do to feel comfortable, but try to remain as motionless as possible.

After about 20 minutes, you are at baseline consciousness in nature. The birds will have gone back to their routines and adjusted to your presence. Other animals may come out now that the birds have relaxed. The birds are truly the guardians of peace, and they accept us in time.

Step 5. Observe the world and your bodily projections, as well as any coincidences that occur outside and inside, like a breeze coming with an image in your mind. These simultaneous expressions are evidence of a growing capacity to participate in nature.

Over time, this simple exercise can deepen, and you will find you can focus quickly and easily during group settings. This is a wonderful way to train the mind to be more accurate with its projections, as well as more sensitive to group dynamics, both human and non-human.

Resources this practice draws from:
Devereux, P. (1996) Revisioning the Earth
Gendlin, E. (1978) Focusing
Young, Jon (1996) Seeing through native eyes: understanding the
              language of nature. 8 CD series.

About the Author

Ryan Hurd is a dream researcher and life-long lucid dreamer. He edits the website DreamStudies.org and lectures internationally about dreams and consciousness. Ryan has a MA in Consciousness Studies and Certificate in Dream Studies from John F. Kennedy University. He also has a BA in Anthropology/Archaeology from the University of GA in Athens and is a member of the International Association for the Study of Dreams.

Endnotes

1	APA Dictionary of Psychology 2007, p. 859.
2	Jong 2005, p. 80.
3	Santomauro and French 2005, p. 672.
4	Dahlitz and Parkes 1993.
5	Yeung, Xu and Chang 2005.
6	Jong, p. 79.
7	LaBerge and Rheingold 1990.
8	Bogzaran, Krippner, and de Carvalho 2002, p. 50.
9	Takeuchi, T. et al. 2002.
10	Santomauro and French, p. 674.
11	Schredl et al. 2009.
12	Van den Bulck 2004. On the other hand, Researcher Jayne Gackenbach (2006) has reported a correlation between gaming and lucid dreams.
13	Hartmann 1984.
14	Fredholm 1999.
15	National Institute of Health, Alcohol and Sleep. http://pubs.niaaa.nih.gov/publications/aa41.htm
16	Lobo and Turik 1997.
17	Zanoli et al. 2005.
18	Barbara Tedlock, invited lecture for the Lucid Art Foundation, February 25, 2006, Pt Reyes, CA
19	NutritionData.com: Foods Highest in Trytophan in Cereal Grains and Pasta
20	McCarty and Chesson 1993.
21	Gangdev 2004.
22	Gangdev
23	Sevilla 2004, p. 70
24	This section is drawn from Sevilla's (2004) longitudinal accounts, as well as from Dahiltz and Parkes 1993, White 2001, Simard and Nielsen 2005, Jong 2005, Lukoff 2007, and McNally and Clancy 2005.
25	Neal-Barnett and Crowther 2000.
26	Cheyne 2001.
27	Sparrow 2006.
28	http://www.rainn.org/statistics

29   "Spiritual emergency" was coined by Stan and
Christine Grof, but Rhea White (2000) is the first to
list it as an "exceptional human experience," while
David Lukoff (2007) lists sleep paralysis as spiritual
emergency and a "visionary spiritual experience."

30   DSM IV 1994, Code V62.89

31   Bill Plotkin, Soulcraft, p. 20.

32   Lukoff 2007.

33   Hufford 2005, p. 37

34   Cheyne et al. 1999.

35   Marquet et al. 1996, cited in Rock 2004, p. 52.

36   Winkelman 2004, p. 60. Neurotheology moves far
beyond this idea and has sponsored some well-meaning
but ultimately reductive quests, such as the search for
the "God gene." Winkelman stays within his warrant
and does not comment on the ontological reality of
spirits, only their phenomenal reality beyond the
cultural source hypothesis which reduces SP visions to
fairy tale replays.

37   Hobson 2002. Hobson and other dream researchers
still debate if REM = dreams, but we can safely say
that most dreams we remember come from this
physiological state.

38   The best introduction to Jung is his autobiography
Memories, Dreams, and Reflections. Hillman book
the *Soul's Code*, while not explicitly about dreams,
showcases his theory of the personality and its inner
workings.

39   Bly 1998.

40   See Chalquist 2007 for more about myth, landscape,
and unconscious acting-out.

41   Sherwood 2002, p. 136. Stan Krippner and Montague's
Ullman's work at the Dream Laboratory of the
Maimonides Medical Center in the 1970s has proven to
be the zenith of scientific work on psychic dreams; but
the evidence is well known to lifelong dreamers.

42   Hunt 1989.

43   Takeuchi et al. 1992. The authors of this study propose
that two thirds of ghost tales, if taken seriously,

	may occur when the witness is in sleep paralysis, highway hypnosis, REM sleep disorder, or other clinically diagnosed diseases and syndromes.
44	Young and Goudet 1994.
45	Sevilla 2000.
46	Tedlock 2001 in Bulkeley's *Dreams: A Reader On The Religious, Cultural, And Psychological Dimensions Of Dreaming.*
47	Devereux 2001, p. 190. Sherwood (2002) also discusses the correlation between hypnagogic hallucinations and anomalous experiences, including telepathy, pyrokinesis, past life experiences, and near death experiences.
48	My apologies to Joseph Campbell, who, to the delight of readers and disdain of academic folklorists everywhere, integrated Jungian psychology with the expressions of folklore, myth, and ritual. See the *Power of Myth.*
49	I don't mean to reduce all uncanny phenomena to physical brain states, such as SP/HH. Rather, I suggest that uncanny states, which sometimes include content that cannot be known by rational means or any psychological process we currently understand, have material correlates. See Proud (2009) for more about the paranormal elements of SP/HH and the spiritist perspective. For a review of the scientific inquiry into psi, ESP and dream telepathy, I recommend Charles Tart's *The End of Materialism.*
50	Hufford 1982, *The Terror That Comes in the Night,* p. 221.
51	Jones 1951, *On the Nightmare,* p. 82. Jones was a student of Freud's and interpreted many SP experiences as repressed sexual urges.
52	Briggs 1976, *Encyclopedia of Fairies.*
53	Froud 1998, *Good Fairies, Bad Fairies.* A whimsical guide, mixed with authentic folklore research and captivating illustrations.
54	Stoker, p. 267 as quoted in Hufford 1982, p 228.
55	Conesa-Sevilla 2004, p. 27.
56	Law and Kirmayer 2005, p. 206

57   Hinton et al. 2005, p. 47.

58   Vatta et al. 2002

59   Hinton, p. 68.

60   Cheyne 2001, p. 140.

61   Cheyne and Girard 2004 group what I have termed here as presence, shadow, and intruder into the category of "intruder" and call the "incubus" hallucination the feeling of being choked, strangled, or otherwise feeling uncomfortable pressure on the chest (p. 283). My splitting of these two groups further into presence and shadows is a "folk psychology division" based on my own experiences and the theory of co-creative dream theory that suggests that our conscious intentions and attitude can alter a dream or hallucination at these junctions. It is a preliminary grouping.

62   Conesa-Sevilla 2004, p. 45-46. Quoted with permission from author.

63   Giving forum to the despised is a challenge noted in many religious traditions around the world. For example, see "the suffering servant" passage in the Torah, Isaiah 53.

64   Furuya et al. 2009, p. 235.

65   Cheyne 2001, p. 146.

66   Armstrong 1994, p. 137, as quoted in Cheyne, p. 146.

67   "I trembled violently from head to foot, and there was a great sound as of many storms colliding, which shook me and threw me on my face. In the moment I was thrown down, I was fully awake and saw how I was thrown down." As quoted in Moss 2010, p. 208. Moss does not link this account to SP, but to dream-visions in general.

68   Mavromatis 1987, p. 100, quoting Swedenborg's *The Word of the Old Testament Explained,* 1746.

69   Hufford 2005.

70   Van De Castle 1994, p. 150.

71   McNally and Clancy 2005.

72   See Forrest 2008 and Sevilla 2004, p. 85. Forrest argues for a correlation with anesthesia awareness, and Sevilla suggests that the encounter could be a mythologized

reliving of medicalized birth trauma. I also wonder about the shadow side of the Western doctor, who dutifully perpetuated terrible crimes against humanity in the last century, including a key role in the theory of eugenics, which led to the forced sterilization of 60,000 American women in the 1930s, as well as the medical atrocities of the Holocaust. See Bruinius 2006.

73   Froud 1998, section titled "IT."

74   Taylor 1992.

75   Bulkeley 2003, p. 7. Dream researchers who clinically study PTSD have reached consensus on the point that PTSD nightmares can be healing, and like other nightmares, the function seems to be to integrate traumatic experiences with other aspects of the dreamer's life.

76   Sherwood, p. 139.

77   Moody 1975.

78   Nelson et al. 2006. A critical response to this "neurological intrusion" was made by Long and Holden in 2007, citing irregularities in Nelson's methodology. However, it is clear the NDE community is threatened by the possibility of a biological correlate to NDE, even though this correlate does not necessarily unauthenticate the transpersonal experiences themselves, just as the transpersonal elements of SP/HH are not invalidated by understanding their association with REM sleep. These are separate fields of inquiry that cannot invalidate each other's premises; they can only complement each other in an interdisciplinary spirit of inquiry.

79   See Ring 1994, Atwater 1992, and Grayson and Bush 1992 for more about the fascinating world of distressing NDEs.

80   Conesa-Sevilla 2004, p. 21.

81   Blackmore 1991.

82   Hufford 2005, p. 38.

83   Kellogg 1989. Lucid dreamer Ed Kellogg actively tries to disregard all beliefs in the lucid dream state. This is also a central aim in the Western philosophical practice of phenomenology.

84   LaBerge et al. 1981.
85   Bogzaran 1990.
86   Hurd 2009.
87   Winkelman 2000. Winkelman does not mean that
            lucid dreamers are shaman, but that they are getting
            their toes wet in a deep pool that is shared by
            contemporary shamanic practitioners, as well as our
            own ancestors in the dawn of human consciousness.
88   See Mindell 1993 and Krippner et al. 2002.
89   A variation of Carlos Casteneda's method in his (1974)
            Journey to Ixtlan.
90   Hurd 2008. This was the subject of my MA thesis,
            an auto-phenomenology into the topic of spontaneous
            emergence in lucid dreaming. In those dreams, I
            frequently emerged spontaneously in a childhood
            setting, where I was given profound opportunities to
            experience fears, anger, sadness, love, and forgiveness
            within family-of-origin settings.
91   Chambers 1999 p. 43.
92   http://jungian.info/library.cfm?idsLibrary=9
93   Hinton et al., p. 52. In this study, a group of
            Cambodian refugees, 67% of their patients with Post-
            Traumatic Stress Disorder, also experienced SP at least
            once a year.
94   See Patricia Garfield's work with lucid sexuality:
            Pathway To Ecstasy.
95   Proud 2009, p. 129.
96   Mavromatis 1987, p. 4.
97   Hunt 1989, p. 180
98   Barrett 2001.
99   Mavromatis, p. 186.
100   Barrett interview 2001.
101   Hillman 1979. When we undergo a conscious trip
            into dreaming, we are activating the archetypal myth
            (or meme, or schema, if you like) of the hero's journey,
            and specifically, the hero's descent into the underworld.
            You will be challenged; you may succeed, or you
            undergo ritual destruction, but either way, you will

return to the surface forever changed, and possibly reborn. As Jung wrote, "one does not become enlightened by imagining figures of light, but by making the darkness conscious. The latter procedure, however, is disagreeable and therefore not popular." *Collected Works 13: Alchemical Studies,* par 335, p. 265.

102	Yuschak 2007.
103	LaBerge 2003.
104	www.spiritualmentoring.com
105	Conesa-Sevilla 2004, pp. 158-159.
106	Kohls and Walash 2007.
107	Young 1996.

References and Bibliography

American Psychiatric Association. (1994). *Diagnostic and statistical manual, fourth edition.* Washington, D.C.

American Psychological Association. (2007). *Dictionary of Psychology.* Gary VandenBos, ed. Washington, D.C.

Armstrong, K. (1994). *A history of God: the 4000 year quest of Judaism, Christianity, and Islam.* New York: Alfred Knopt.

Atwater, P. (1992). Is there a Hell? Surprising observations about near-death experience. *Journal of Near-Death Studies,* 10(3), pp. 149-160.

Barrett, D. (2001). *Committee of Sleep.* New York: Crown Publishers.

Barrett, D. (2001). Interview found at http://www.spiritofmaat. com/archive/may3/barrett.htm

Blackmore, S. (1991). Lucid dreams and OBEs. *Lucidity.* 10(1&2), pp. 107 – 117.

Bly, R. (1988). *A little book on the human shadow.* New York: HarperOne.

Bogzaran, F. (2005). Dreaming mind and creative mind. *Shift,* March-May, No.6, Institute of Noetic Sciences.

Briggs, K. (1976). *Encyclopedia of fairies: hobgoblins, brownies, bogies, and other supernatural creatures.* New York: Penguin Books.

Bruinius, H. (2006). *Better for all the world: the secret history of forced sterilization and America's quest for racial purity.* New York: Alfred Knopf.

Bulkeley, K. (2003). *Dreams of healing*. New York: Paulist Press.

Bulkeley, K. (2005). *The wondering brain*. New York: Routledge.

Campbell, J. and Moyers, B. (1988). *The power of myth*. New York: Doubleday.

Chalquist, C. (2007). *Terrapsychology: reengaging the soul of place*. New Orleans: Spring Journal Books.

Chambers, P. (1999). *Sex and the paranormal*. London: Blandford.

Cheyne, J.A. and Girard, T.A. (2004). Spatial characteristics of hallucinations associated with sleep paralysis. *Cognitive Neuropsychiatry*, 9(4), pp. 281-300.

Cheyne, J.A, Rueffer, S.D., and Newby-Clarke. (1999). Hypnagogic and hypnopompic hallucinations during sleep paralysis: neurological and cultural construction of the nightmare. *Consciousness and cognition*, 8, pp. 319-337.

Cheyne, J.A. (2001). The ominous numinous: sensed presence and 'other' hallucinations. *Journal of Consciousness Studies*, 8, no 5-7, pp. 133-150.

Conesa-Sevilla, J. (2000). Geomagnetic, cross-cultural and occupational faces of sleep paralysis: and ecological perspective. *Sleep and Hypnosis*, 2, pp. 105-111.

Conesa-Sevilla, J. (2004). *Wrestling with ghosts: a personal and scientific account of sleep paralysis*. Xlibris/Randomhouse.

Dahlitz, M. and Parkes, J.D. (1993). Sleep paralysis. *Lancet*, 341(8842), p. 406-07.

Devereux, P. (2001). *Haunted land: investigations into ancient mysteries and modern day phenomena.* London: Piatkus.

Forrest, D. (2008). Alien abduction: a medical hypothesis. *Journal of the American Academy of Psychoanalysis and Dynamic Psychiatry,* Fall 2008, 36(3), pp. 431-441.

Fredholm, B., Battig, K., Holmen, J., Nehlig, A., Zvartau, E. (1999). Actions of caffeine in the brain with special reference to factors that contribute to its widespread use. *Pharmacological Reviews,* March 1, 1999, 51(1), pp. 83-133.

Froud, B. (1998). *Good fairies, bad fairies.* New York: Simon and Schuster.

Furuya, H., Ikezoe, K., Shigeto, H., Oyyagi, Y., Arahata, H., Araki, E., and Fujii, N. (2009). Sleep- and non-sleep-related hallucinations—relationship to ghost tales. *Dreaming,* 19(4), December 2009, pp. 232-238.

Gackenbach, J. (2006). Video game play and lucid dreams: implications for the development of consciousness. *Dreaming,* 16, pp. 96-110.

Gangdev, P. (2004). Relevance of sleep paralysis and hypnic hallucinations to psychiatry. *Australian Psychiatry,* 12(1), pp. 77-80.

Garfield, P. (1979). *Pathway to ecstasy: the way of the dream mandala.* Austin: Holt Rinehart and Winston.

Grayson, B., and Bush, N.E. (1992). Distressing near-death experiences, *Psychiatry,* 55, pp. 95-110.

Grof, S. and Grof, C. (1989). eds, *Spiritual emergency: when personal transformation becomes a crisis.* Los Angeles: Tarcher.

Hartmann, E. (1984). *The nightmare: the psychology and biology of terrifying dreams.* New York: Basic Books.

Hillman, J. (1979). *The dream and the underworld.* New York: Harper & Row.

Hillman, J. (1996). *The soul's code: in search of character and calling.* New York: Random House.

Hinton, D., Pich, V., Chhean, D., and Pollack, M. (2005). The ghost pushes you down: sleep paralysis-type panic attacks in a Khmer refugee population. *Transcultural Psychiatry*, 42(1), pp. 46-77.

Hobson, J.A. (2002) *Dreaming: an introduction to the science of sleep.* Oxford University Press.

Hufford, D. (1982). *The terror that comes in the night.* Philadelphia: University of Pennsylvania Press.

Hufford, D. (2005). Sleep paralysis as spiritual experience. *Transcultural Psychiatry*, 41(1), pp. 11-45.

Hunt, H. (1989). *The multiplicity of dreams.* New Haven: Yale University.

Hurd, R. (2008). *Spontaneous emergence: a phenomenology of lucid dreaming.* MA thesis, May 2008, John F. Kennedy University.

Hurd, R. (2009). Lucid nightmares: the dark side of lucid dreaming. Presentation at the Annual Conference for the International Study of Dreams, Chicago, IL. Audio at http://dreamstudies.org/2009/09/28/lucid-nightmare-podcast/

Jones, E. (1951). *On the nightmare.* New York: Liveright Publishing Corp.

Jong, J.T. (2005). Cultural variation in the clinical presentation of sleep paralysis. *Transcultural psychiatry.* 42(1), pp. 78- 92.

Jung, C. (1961). *Memories, dreams and reflections.* Aniele Jaffe (ed), New York: Random House.

Kellogg, E.W.III. (1989). Mapping territories: a phenomenology of lucid dream reality. *Lucidity Letter* 8(2), pp. 81-97.

Kezler, K. (1987). *The sun and the shadow: my experiment with lucid dreaming.* Virginia Beach: A.R.E. Press.

Kohls and Walash. (2007). Psychological distress, experiences of ego loss and spirituality: exploring the effects of spiritual practice. *Social behavior and personality.* 35(10), pp. 1301-1316.

Krippner, S. Bogzaran, F., and de Carvalho, A. (2002). *Extraordinary dreams and how to work them.* Albany: SUNY Press.

LaBerge, S. Nagel. L., Dement, W.C., and Zarcone, V. (1981). Lucid dreaming verified by volitional communication during REM sleep. *Psychophysiology,* 20, pp. 454-455.

LaBerge, S. and Rheingold, H. (1990). *Exploring the world of lucid dreaming.* New York: Ballantine.

LaBerge, S. (2003). Substances that enhance recall and lucidity during dreaming, *United States Patent Application 604138.*

Law, S. and Kirmayer, L., (2005). Inuit interpretations of sleep paralysis. *Transcultural Psychiatry,* 42(1), pp. 93-112.

Lobo, L. and Turik, S. (1997). Effects of alcohol on sleep parameters of sleep-deprived healthy volunteers, *Sleep,* 20(1), pp. 52-59.

Long, J. and Holden, J. (2007). Does the arousal system contribute to near-death and out-of-body experiences? A summary and response. *Journal of Near Death Experience*, 25(3), pp. 136-169.

Lukoff, D. (2007). Visionary spiritual experiences, *Southern Medical Journal,* 100(6), pp. 635-641.

McCarty, D. and Chesson, A. (2009). A Case of Sleep Paralysis with Hypnopompic Hallucinations, *Journal of Clinical Sleep Medicine*, February 15; 5(1): 83–84.

McNally, R. and Clancy, S. (2005). Sleep paralysis, sexual abuse, and space alien abduction. *Transcultural Psychiatry*, 42(1), pp. 113-122.

Marquet, P., Peters, J., Delfiore, G., Degueldre, C., Luxen, A., and Franck, G. (1996). Functional neuroanatomy of human rapid-eye-movement sleep and dreaming, *Nature* 383, pp. 163-166.

Mavromatis, A. (1987). *Hypnagogia: the unique state of consciousness between wakefulness and sleep.* London: Routledge & Kegan Paul.

Mindell, A. (1993). *The shaman's body.* San Francisco: Harper.

Moss, R. (2010). *Dreamgates: exploring the worlds of soul, imagination and life beyond death.* Novato: New World Library.

Moody, R.A., Jr. (1975). *Life after life.* Covington: Mockingbird Press.

Neal-Barnett, A. and Crowther, J. (2000). To be female, middle class, anxious, and black. *Psychology of Women Quarterly.* 24, pp. 129-136.

Nelson, K., Mattingly, M., Lee, S., and Schmitt, F. (2006). Does the arousal system contribute to near-death experience? *Neurology*, 66(1), pp. 1003-1009.

Paradis, C. and Friedman, S. (2005). Sleep paralysis in African-Americans with panic disorder. *Transcultural Psychiatry*, 42(1), pp. 123-134.

Plotkin, B. (2003). *Soulcraft: crossing into the mysteries of nature and psyche.* Novato: New World Library.

Proud, L. (2009). *Dark intrusions: An investigation into the paranormal nature of sleep paralysis experiences.* San Antonio: Anomalist Books.

Ring, K. (1994). Solving the riddle of frightening near-death experiences, *Journal of Near-Death Studies*, 13(1), pp. 5-23.

Rock, A. (2004). *The mind at night: the new science of how and why we dream.* New York: Basic Books.

Santomauro, J. and French, C. (2009). Terror in the night. *The Psychologist* 22(8), August, pp. 672-675.

Schredl, M., Atamasova, D., Hormann, K., Maurer, J., Hummell, T., and Stuck, B. (2009). Information processing during sleep: the effect of olfactory stimuli on dream content and dream emotions. *Journal of Sleep Research*, 18(3), pp. 285 – 290.

Sherwood, S. (2002). Relationship between the hypnagogic/hynogogic states and reports of anomalous experiences. *Journal of parapsychology*, 66, pp. 127-150.

Simard, V. and Nielsen, T. (2005). Sleep paralysis—associated sensed presence as a possible manifestation of social anxiety. *Dreaming*, Vol. 15(4), pp. 245-260.

Sparrow, S. (2006). The five star method: a process-oriented, competency-based approach to dream interpretation. Paper presented at the *Annual Conference for the International Association for the Study of Dreams*, Bridgewater, MA.

Takeuchi, T., Miyasita, A., Inugami, M., Sasaki, Y., and Fukuda, K. (1992). Isolated sleep paralysis elicited by sleep interruption. *Sleep*, 15, pp. 217-225.

Takeuchi, T., Miyasita, Y., Sasaki, Y., Inugami, M., and Fuluda, K. (1993). Laboratory-documented hallucination during sleep-onset REM period in a normal subject. *Perceptual and Motor Skills*, 78(217), pp. 225

Takeuchi. T., Fukuda, K., Sasaki, Y., Inugami, M., and Murphy, T. (2002). Factors related to the occurrence of isolated sleep paralysis elicited during a multi-phase sleep-wake schedule. *Sleep*, 25, 1, pp. 89-96.

Tart, C. (2009). *The end of materialism: how evidence for the paranormal is bringing science and spirit together.* Oakland: New Harbinger Publications.

Taylor, J. (1992). *Where people fly and water runs uphill.* New York: Warner Books.

Tedlock, B. (2001). The new anthropology of dreaming. In Kelly Bulkeley (ed) *Dreams: a reader on the religious, cultural and psychological dimensions of dreaming*, New York: Palgrave, pp. 249-264,.

Tedlock, B. (2005). *The Woman in the Shaman's Body. Reclaiming the Feminine in Religion and Medicine.* NY: Bantam Books.

Van den Bulch, J. (2004). Media Use and Dreaming: The Relationship Among Television Viewing, Computer Game Play, and Nightmares or Pleasant Dreams. *Dreaming*, Vol 14(1), March 2004, pp. 43-49.

Van De Castle, R. (1994). *Our dreaming mind.* New York: Ballantine Books.

Vatta, M., Durmaine, R., Varghese, G., Richard, T.A., Shimizu, W., Aihara, N., Nademanee, K., Brugada, R., Brugada, J., Veerakul, G., Li, H., Bowles, N.E., Brugada, P., Antzelevitch, C., and Towbin, J.A. (2002). Genetic and biophysical basis of sudden unexplained nocturnal death syndrome (SUNDS), a disease allelic to Brugada syndrome. *Human Molecular Genetics*, 11(3), pp. 337-45.

Waggoner, R. (2009). *Lucid dreaming: gateway to the inner self.* Needham: Moment Point Press.

Whalen, P.J. (1998). Fear, vigilance, and ambiguity: initial neuroimaging studies of the human amygdala, *Current Directions in Psychological Science*, 7, pp. 177-188.

White, R. (2000). *List of extraordinary human experiences. http://www.ehe.org*

Winkelman, M. (2004). Spirits as human nature and the fundamental structures of consciousness, in James Houran (Ed) *Shaman to scientist.* Lanham, MD: Scarecrow Press, pp. 59-96.

Young, D. and Gouley, J.G., Eds. (1994). *Being Changed: The Anthropology of Extraordinary Experience.* Ontario, Canada: Broadview Press.

Young, J. 1996. *Seeing through native eyes.* Owl Media.

Yeung, Xu and Chang (2005). Prevalence and illness beliefs of sleep paralysis among Chinese psychiatric patients in China and the United States. *Transcultural psychiatry*, 42(1), pp. 135-144.

Yuschak, T. (2007). *Pharmalogical induction of lucid dreams.* Downloaded 8/2008.

Zanoli, P., Rivasi, M., Zavattit, M., Brusiani, F., and Baraldi, M. (2005). New insight into the neuropharmacological activity of *Humulus lupulus* L. *Journal of Ethnopharmacology,* Vol 102, Issue 1, 31 October, pp. 102-106

Index

A

B

C

D

E

F

S

Spiritual emergency 3, 28, 29, 75, 94, 103
Spiritual practices 81, 82
SSRIs 22
Succubus 41, 70
Surrender 4, 27, 67
"Swedenborg, Emmanuel" 53, 97

T

Threat vigilance system 36
Tryptophan 21

V

Vampires 42, 45, 72
Video games 16
Visitations of the dead 51
Vortex 68, 69, 78, 79, 81

W

Wake-initiated sleep paralysis 78
White noise 16
Witchcraft 41

Y

Yohimbe 22

Made in the USA
Middletown, DE
07 September 2016